OWNERSHIP versus HIERARCHY
The Choice of The Dominant Method

SIMON BRANZBURG

Table of Contents

Introduction

The documented history of humanity is the history of mixing two methods of interaction and cooperation between humans: **Hierarchy and Ownership**, the former supporting top-down control over resources and the latter supporting control distributed between the Owners. Historically Hierarchy method had always been dominant, with the Ownership method being quite limited. The time has come to settle this struggle into the new accommodation. I believe that this accommodation should include the dominance of Ownership, especially Ownership of Self, with Hierarchy, used sparingly, and only when it is indispensable.

This essay aims to insert into discussion some specific suggestions for change in the balance between Hierarchy and Ownership in such a way that it would be most favorable for the pursuit of happiness by each individual as this individual understands it. The essential suggestion is to recognize, as individual property equally belonging to everybody, the Common Inheritance of know-how, narratives, language, and communication skills that constitute the specific culture. After that, it would become possible to establish a process of compensation for the use of this property that would guarantee sufficient, even if unequal, returns on this property to individuals, not willing or unable to use it effectively, by others who are willing and able to use it effectively. These returns had to be unequal because, as with any other form of property, they will depend on the ability of individuals to manage it more or less efficiently.

First of all, let's define what we are talking about here:

Hierarchy is a form of interaction and cooperation between humans when one human, designated as superior, can direct another - inferior, using coercion and violence as needed. In a group of humans with two or more individuals, everybody is assigned formally or informally to some position in a hierarchical pyramid. In this pyramid, some people are below others, some above, and some at the same level. Control over resources, including bodies of members of the Hierarchy, is concentrated at the top as much as possible and used to satisfy superior individuals' physiological and psychological needs. Only technical ability to process information, issue directives, obtain truthful feedback on these directives' implementation and apply corrective measures limit this control. Another considerable limitation is the psychological conditions of inferiors who may or may not comply with directions from superiors even under the risk of physical and mental punishment. Typical examples would be patriarchal family, military, government, or corporate hierarchies.

Ownership is a form of interaction and cooperation between humans when each individual has some recognized set of resources, first of all, one's own body, completely under their control. Owners use this control to satisfy their physiological and psychological needs either directly or via voluntary cooperation and exchanging goods and services with others. This control is limited only by possible interference by others if they find an individual's use of such power causes conflict with their control over their resources and bodies and therefore requires some reconciliation. Other than that, no use of coercion or violence occurs. Typical examples would be a group of hunter-gatherers, family, either nuclear or in any other form, based on equality of adult members, business partnership based on voluntary cooperation, a team of specialists with diverse skill sets voluntary cooperating on a project, and so on.

This essay consists of 5 parts:

Part I: Methods of Interaction

This part reviews the nature of production and its components, two methods of Human Interaction and cooperation used symbiotically in production, and their plusses and minuses.

Part II: The Challenge of Human Redundancy and Suggested Solution

This part reviews how these methods developed and how this development led to the challenge of **THE CONSTANTLY INCREASING REDUNDANCY OF HUMAN LABOR FOR PRODUCING GOODS AND SERVICES.** It also suggests the process to nullify the negative impact of this redundancy by recognizing an individual share of the Common Inheritance of the Nation as a tradable asset.

Part III: Relevant Parts of Underlying World View

Part III is about my understanding of humans and their groups based on the belief that their development is a complex evolutionary process. A human individual's genes and epigenetics are the only units of evolutionary selection with dual features: some benefiting group survival over individual survival and some benefiting individual survival over the group. The dynamic combination of these features is necessary because individuals cannot survive without belonging to a group. Similarly, without taking care of Self, individuals could not survive either.

Part IV: Conceptual Understanding of Previous Development.

Part IV presents my understanding of humanity's development process, which is the cumulative process when humans increasingly control the environment while human efforts required for resources acquisition are constantly decreasing.

Part V: Conceptual Understanding of Future Development Alternatives

Part V presents my understanding of the future continuation of the development process described in Part IV, which could take one of two directions: more beneficial for the human pursuit of happiness and more detrimental to this activity.

A very brief word about the author of this essay: I spent the first 37 years of my life as a citizen of the Union of Soviet <u>Socialist</u> Republics (USSR) and then the next 30+ years in the United States of America (USA), initially as a legal immigrant and then as a citizen. In both places, I obtained education at the graduate level and decades of professional experience as a systems engineer and business systems consultant, which exposed me to a wide range of people, businesses, and information processes in both countries. So, my understanding of reality based on this experience with the internal workings of these two systems analyzed in conjunction with ideas and information from many other sources.

Part I. Methods of Interaction

Nature of Production and Distribution of Goods and Services

Components Used in Production

1.	**Common Inheritance**. The most important component used in production not only by any group of people, but each individual is the Common Inheritance that consists of the totality of environmental inputs that define the content of every individual's mind. Unlike computer hardware, a BioWare of the brain constantly changes its material structure from the moment of its initial formation months before birth until the end of life. Thus, the essential process in an individual's development is acquiring non-material artifacts that define how this individual interacts with other people and the environment: the language, rules of interaction and behavior, and variety of skills necessary for at least minimally effective functioning.

For example, an individual raised in a group with a culture optimized for desert would not survive without help in the rainforest. Similarly, an individual from the rainforest would have a hard time in the desert. At the same time, both of them would have a hard time living in the contemporary city. Since these non-material artifacts are common for everybody, their use is accessible to all even if the intensity and effectiveness of such use vary greatly. This Common Inheritance that individuals acquire through birth and later inclusion into some society is pretty much analogous to a computer operating system that directly controls hardware and is the base of functionality without which no computer can function.

2.	**Human Capital: Cognitive and Manual.** The second most crucial production component is specific skills and knowledge, which an individual develops via education and practical activities. These are particular conditions of the brain's BioWare relevant for conducting productive activities, which are highly specific to an individual and not easily transferrable to anybody else. These skills and knowledge represent truly unalienable Human Capital. External control over Human Capital with a whip or carrot results in severe limitation on its productive use. It could even be counterproductive in case of active resistance. Human Capital is never free and typically provides its owners' returns obtained either via labor market in Ownership system or via allocation from superiors in Hierarchical System. One interesting point is that, even when the Hierarchical system was slavery, slaveowners had to allocate more resources to individuals with higher levels of Human Capital. Otherwise, the slave in control of this Capital will deny to slaveowner effective use of such Capital. Human Capital as a production component is analogous to Application software, which works on the top of the Operating system and provides specific functionality for any task, whether this task requires the use of Human Cognitive Capital to handle symbols or the Human Manual Capital to handle materials.

3. **Material Capital.** The third and relatively less critical component includes all material artifacts, whether raw materials and infrastructure, buildings and machines, patents and blueprints, or whatever else that could be used in production and situated outside the human brain and body. Material Capital is analogous to computer hardware: it is necessary for producing goods and services but does not define their forms and processes. This component is of relatively low importance compared to the first two components because the low level of Material Capital or even its limitation to raw materials provided by the Environment does not prevent production, only makes it less efficient. Without the first two components, the goods and services would be impossible to produce in any conceivable environment.

The 1st component - Common Inheritance, would assure effective communications and interactions between people. At least one individual in possession of the 2nd component - Human Capital appropriate for the given environment, both Cognitive and Manual, would allow production albeit at the lower level of productivity. Finally, access to the 3^{d} component - Material Capital is also required but could be helpful only if the first two components are in place.

Development of Production Processes

Throughout the history of humanity, humans used all three components combined in production. However, the first component – Common Inheritance constantly changes, increasing in complexity and causing changes in relative weight and value of other parts. It defines the functionality of the second component – Human Capital and the usefulness of the third component – Material Capital while remaining unrecognizable and invisible like water is invisible for fish and air for birds.

Until recently, the second component – Human Capital, was continuously rising in value mainly based on specialization. However, this improvement was slow and primarily limited to fighting abilities for a while. Levels of productivity remained relatively constant, so one needed more bodies to do more. Then, quite recently, humanity hit the wall of the Industrial Revolution when the use of machines started the devaluation of Human Manual Capital. Even more recently, the Information Revolution initiated the devaluation of Human Cognitive Capital.

The third component – Material Capital, while not the most important for production, is the most visible, recognizable, and controllable, resulting in constant competition, including military, between individuals and groups for control over it.

As long as humans were hunter-gatherers and obtained resources directly from the environment, resource quantification wasn't needed. Afterward, Humanity developed two methods of human interaction and cooperation: Hierarchy and Ownership, which allowed much more effective division of labor and coordination of human activities. This development was forced on humans by consequences of their expansion all over the planet and the resulting competition for resources between groups. The winners were the groups that developed more effective processes of using production components, making such groups more competitive technologically and militarily. Since nothing ever stay the same and changes are inevitable, even if sometimes slow and barely visible, it led to the constant reshuffling, merging, raising, and falling of some societies and cultures at the expense of others. Before we move any further, let's examine these two methods of human interaction and cooperation in detail.

Hierarchy vs. Ownership: Symbiotic Use of Methods

Any method of human action to achieve its objectives consists of some general rules of the game applied to interactions between individuals. These rules define all crucial processes:

- The process of the definition of desirable objectives,
- The method of data collection about the environment,
- The process of acting within a given environment,
- The process of feedback from the environment. This process shows whether these actions achieved expected results or not.

All of these processes work differently for Hierarchy and Ownership. However, in reality, both these methods are used symbiotically when the dominant approach is used by default while being supported by the alternative method when the dominant could not provide at least a minimally effective outcome of actions.

Rules of Game

Any group of humans, either small or huge, using some formal Hierarchy or informal network of Ownership, has to have some generally accepted rules of the game. These rules limit the behavior of individuals, so, in case of consistent violation of these rules, they could be either excluded from the group, contained, or just eliminated.

These rules are applied differently within each method. Thus, for example, in the case of Hierarchy, even if formal laws are the same for everybody, they are used differently depending on people's position in Hierarchy. The objective is to keep an individual's behavior within limits designated for this individual's specific station in Hierarchy. In the case of Ownership, rules are the same for everybody, and the objective is to protect individuals' control over resources owned.

Correspondingly societies with the dominance of Hierarchy are lawless – the law is what the superior says at any given moment. Therefore, people had to appeal to higher superiors in the Hierarchy to resolve any conflict. In contrast, societies with Ownership dominance had to be based on the rule of law because its members could maintain their status as owners only via negotiated, commonly accepted, and stable processes that support satisfactory reconciliation of conflicting interests.

The reality never provides a perfect example of a society with exclusive use of one method only. Probably the only exceptions are groups of hunter-gatherers too small for establishing formal hierarchy, which had minimal use of material components of production, making ownership of the second component – human capital the dominant form. Correspondingly, the law expressed as the tradition was the dominant factor in defining the rules in these societies. Nevertheless, history provides two recent examples of the overwhelming dominance of one method:

- The totalitarian socialism in the Soviet Union under Stalin with the dominance of Hierarchy
- The United States until the end of the frontier, when the agricultural society of Ownership with practically unlimited access to the land, provided property sufficient for material independence.

Each of these relatively recent cases produced distinctive types of Rules of the game:

- The Soviet Union, dominated by the Hierarchy, produced the rule of bosses from the top down, with a law being nothing more than a propaganda tool and traditions for all practical purposes eliminated. This society had a minuscule number of lawyers and a tremendous number of Communist Party apparatchiks promoting directives from the top down and multiplying such commands at each level of Hierarchy where some individuals within Hierarchy would decide every issue. People had to appeal to the Central Committee of the Communist Party to resolve any dispute. This appeal would slowly move down to the resolution level, where a local bureaucrat would decide supporting which side would be most beneficial for his career.
- The United States, with its strong presence of the Ownership method, produced the rule of law, even if it was far from perfect. It was initially established mainly at the local level when judges controlled by the local population decided disputes according to common law and traditions of local people, while minuscule numbers of political apparatchiks were fighting each other for support of the people, at least to the extent of not rebelling against rigged election results, and, when in power, sucked up a relatively small share of resources extracted from population and modified rules of the game to benefit their supporters within limits of established laws and traditions.

Eventually, both extremes proved to be unsustainable:

- The Soviet Union, with its nearly exclusive use of the Hierarchy method, fell apart due to its inability to produce sufficient amounts of quality goods and services, opening lots of space for the use of the Ownership method, even if the Hierarchy method remains dominant.

- Historically, very unusual and temporary dominance of the Ownership method in the United States produced an abundance of quality goods and services but rendered a significant share of the population redundant for this production. This part of the population could not obtain adequate resource allocation within the framework of the Ownership method. It successfully fought and achieved the significant diminishment of the Ownership method and dramatic increase in the use of the Hierarchy method, albeit with American specificity: more courts, judges, and lawyers acting more like political apparatchiks without any regard to the constitution or written laws. Another part of redundant people found a good place within more distinct hierarchy method areas: government bureaucracy and big business. Together these members of the Hierarchy are constantly interfering with the use of the Ownership method, limiting but not eliminating it.

Now let's look at the expression of these rules of the game in specific functional processes.

Definition of Objectives

The reality is that whatever formal objectives any group of people pursues, the real goals are to meet the physiological and psychological needs of individuals who define these formal objectives. Thus, the essential difference between Hierarchy and Ownership as methods of interaction and cooperation is who makes decisions impacting an individual's life. In Hierarchy, people at the top make most decisions for the vast majority of people based on the control over resources from the top down. The people at the top usually pretend that they do it for the benefit of some abstraction: either "people" or "state" or "nation" or "our business" or whatnot, and they apply resources in the name of this abstraction.

Such ideological substitution of the actual beneficiary with abstraction allows individuals at the top of the Hierarchy to use individuals at the lower levels as means to their ends. But, of course, to obtain acceptance from individuals at lower levels of Hierarchy, people at the top had to instill in the minds of these individuals the belief that, being a part of the abstraction, they will also benefit. However, since the realities of life constantly remind people that it is not the case, the vast propaganda effort is necessary for maintaining the confusion.

Whether this propaganda effort is sufficient for individuals at the bottom to really accept and support presented objectives is relevant only to the extent that tools of coercion and violence available to people at the top are sufficient to cover the gap that exists between required and actual beliefs of individuals at the lower levels and forces their compliance. Thus, the critical consequence of objectives set by people at the top is the proliferation of large projects directed to satisfy the psychological needs of these people combined with the general disregard of the needs of individuals at the bottom. Historically there are well-documented cases when the levels of neglect were such that millions of people died from starvation.

In Ownership, adult individuals make most decisions for their own benefits based on resources available to each individual, which is always unequal. However, the resources applied are unnecessarily limited because many individuals could pull the resources together to achieve common objectives. This pulling of resources occurs from the bottom up. It never includes all people's resources, but a somewhat different share of resources from some individuals and none from others. Because in Ownership method of interaction and cooperation tools of coercion and violence are not available, the effort is directed at convincing people that they benefit, at least psychologically, from allocating their resources to achieve proposed objectives. The abstractions are still helpful in this environment, but not that much.

Unlike Hierarchy, Ownership means that resources are distributed, so when proponents of something use the propaganda to promote it, the opponents of this something have resources for the counter-propaganda campaign. So, it is tough to achieve a high level of resource concentration without providing a straightforward and clear answer for everybody to the question, "What's in it for me?"

Consequently, people in a society with Ownership dominance seldom allocate resources to any large unprofitable project because it is hard to convince a sufficient number of people to support it. It is even more challenging to implement some symbolic use of resources with little to no benefits for regular people.

Technically it means that in Hierarchy, decision-makers at the top extract resources from all and then allocate them to satisfy their own needs and wants. On the other hand, in Ownership, individuals provide their resources unequally based on their unequal expectations of returns resources. Once again, the actual historical example is very instructive. The Soviet Union, with its dominance of the Hierarchy method, allocated vast amounts of resources to a multitude of economically meaningless massive projects and the symbolic use of resources such as building monuments to Stalin, Lenin, and others. It also made monumental buildings for top-level people to work in, expensive housing to live in, and luxurious recreational retreats, all of these unavailable to the individuals at the bottom.

The United States, on the other hand, when they were a society with dominant Ownership method, had very little of this – one can quickly check the story of building White House, or Capitol, or Washington monument. However, it changed when the growing political and bureaucratic class started substituting the Ownership method with

Hierarchy on the mass scale in the 1930s. The monuments and monumental buildings start growing like mushrooms after a good rain. So, if somebody unfamiliar with the central part of Washington or Moscow suddenly placed there, he would have difficulty finding differences in style, manner, or cost wasted between the monstrosities created by Soviet Socialist Hierarchy and American quasi-Capitalist Hierarchy.

Data Collection:

Data collection about the environment is a necessary component of any activity. However, like everything else, it is done very differently depending on which method of interaction and cooperation is used. For example, in Hierarchy, the process is indirect with many intermediaries, while in Ownership, the process is direct with no intermediaries involved. Each of these methods has advantages and disadvantages.

The significant advantage of Hierarchy is that its coercive ability allows forced collection of data about anything and everything regardless of the cost of such data collection. Moreover, this advantage guarantees that individuals at the top levels of Hierarchy could demand any information they deem necessary for decision making. On the negative side, however, this neglect of the cost of data collection leads to consumption of the unordinary amount of resources, distracting people from their productive activities, and often is severely distorted by all these intermediaries who adjust data to obtain maximum benefits for themselves. In short: if you can kill the messenger, do not expect to receive the undistorted message.

The significant advantage of the Ownership method is that collected data is undistorted as long as they are observable by the Owner, who has all incentives for obtaining truthful information. On the negative side, the data collection, in this case, is limited not only by scope but also by the Owner's ability to check the validity of collected data due to the cost and difficulties of such process. However, there is an excellent, naturally developed way to collect data from many sources and relatively cheaply while generally assuring the validity of these data. This way of data collection occurs through the exchange of goods and services via the marketplace without price controls and other forced regulations. In this case, most of the necessary information is included in the price, so Owners can direct resources to satisfy the needs of people according to their preference expressed via readiness to pay or not for goods and services offered. However, this process includes a necessary form of cultural evolution leading to inequality: Owners good at extracting valid data from various market and cultural signals expand their ownership of resources at the expense of Owners that fail in this activity.

Actions

Human actions occur the same way in any system: individuals act to satisfy their physiological and psychological needs. However, methods of interaction and

13

cooperation provide different drivers for individuals to perform well: Hierarchy uses instilled beliefs, coercion, and violence, causing the primary driver of individual action to be adverse: strive to avoid harm either psychological for not complying with ideal or physical as a result of coercion and violence. Generally, except for true believers who usually get punished at least psychologically for recognizing the gap between beliefs and reality, the best way to satisfy needs is to comply with directions and avoid any initiative that could upset superiors. Since a Hierarchy member gets resources allocated according to position rather than productivity, the best strategy is to do nothing beyond standard requirements. Because the Ownership method is based on voluntary cooperation, the main driver of individual action is positive: strive to achieve something that would provide additional resources according to individual's ambition, rather than the station in Hierarchy. This something has to be some productive activity because, unlike Hierarchy, in the Ownership method, you get nothing if you produce nothing.

Another essential point of difference is the initiation of action. In Hierarchy, individuals' actions, except for a few individuals at the top, are initiated by somebody else. In Ownership, the person who started some activities implements them in reality. This difference creates fascinating dynamics. In Hierarchy, because separation of initiation of action and its actual implementation is typical for this method, individuals design steps poorly, carry them on without enthusiasm, and, in case of ineffective action, continue long after the acting individual recognizes the futility of this action. On the other hand, the unity of initiation of action and its actual implementation in the Ownership method forces an individual to think it through more carefully and implement it enthusiastically. Also, in case of ineffective action, stop it as soon as ineffectiveness becomes evident to avoid unnecessary expenditure of resources.

One can use the comparison of the process of industrialization in the United States of the late XIX century and the Soviet Union of the 1930s as a pretty good illustration of these two methods' workings. The USA used the predominantly Ownership method when industrialization was driven from the bottom up by individuals with limited resources producing something more practical and at a better price than competitors, attracting more resources, and eventually building a multitude of production and service facilities. The result was a consumer-driven economy that quite effectively satisfies the needs of people for everything, be it food, housing, or cars.

On the other hand, the USSR used a predominantly Hierarchical method. Communist Party leaders drove industrialization from the top down. These leaders had complete control over all resources of the country. These resources included people's bodies, and leaders sent them wherever they wanted, even if these bodies lasted but a few weeks in this place before dying from starvation and exposure. The result became painfully obvious when the Soviet Union fell apart in 1991. The industrial base built after decades of ruthless effort at the cost of millions of lives turned out to be pretty much good for nothing. Of course, this result is somewhat masked in Russia by the availability of vast oil and gas deposits. Still, it is nakedly clear in the second biggest Soviet republic Ukraine, which was the site of mass industrial build-up in the Soviet period but became one of the world's poorest countries after independence because of its uncompetitive economy.

Feedback

The final step in the cycle - feedback at first glance looks pretty much similar to the data collection, but it is not the same. This process has two crucial differences from the data collection: a much narrower focus of feedback and much more significant consequences. The feedback necessitates the narrow focus due to the limitation of data collection to data that could have a plausible causal relationship with previous actions. The effects of feedback are always significant because they inevitably impact the estimate of the success or failure of prior efforts, forcing decisions about future resource allocation and action, whether to increase, decrease, or keep the same activities and resource allocation under review. As in all other areas, our two methods of interaction and cooperation: Hierarchy and Ownership, demonstrate different patterns of human behavior.

In Hierarchy, feedback is indirect, processed via multiple layers with decreasing impact on the real lives of individuals at higher levels. The people at the top of the Hierarchy make decisions, while people at the bottom experience the actual consequences of these decisions. It also creates an incentive for distortion at each level. Whatever adverse effects of these decisions occur, they will have no impact on the lives of top people. For individuals at the intermediate levels of Hierarchy, such results, even if they experience a negative impact on their lives, pale in comparison with the adverse effects of demonstrating superiors' mistakes or even incompetence. These processes, inherent in Hierarchy, result in slow feedback processing, so any decision to change course implemented over a long time and resources waste continued for a while. At worst, feedback distortion results in actions causing the continuation of incorrect course until the complete crash because individuals at the top do not see it coming. At the same time, individuals at the lower levels are too afraid to provide helpful feedback.

In Ownership, feedback is direct and has an immediate impact on the life and wellbeing of the Owner. Therefore, whatever decision the Owner made and actions applied, the result would impact this Owner, and there is no way to avoid this impact. Indeed, despite the psychological problems in changing the course of action per received feedback, such as sunk costs, undermining self-esteem, and so on, the Owner could ignore feedback only at his own expense, not somebody else.

As usual, history provides many beautiful examples, but I would like to use a minor incident that demonstrates how it works. In the middle of the 1950s, the Soviet communist leader Khrushchev decided that corn was the best crop to raise, so he ordered a dramatic increase in the planting of corn. The "wise" decision went down through Hierarchy, and collective farms planted corn everywhere whether conditions were appropriate or not. The feedback from agricultural professionals and information about the result of initial planting was suppressed, with propaganda media promoting false narratives about the whole process. Somehow, nature refused to comply with the "wise" directions of the top man in the communist Hierarchy, and, as a result, corn did not grow in many places. Since the collective farms did not produce the crops they would typically plant in these areas, it resulted in the bread lines and limitations on consumption. None of these impacted individuals at the top levels of Hierarchy, so the slow process of growing unhappiness of the population, reports about it by the secret police, and even open protests required to correct the problem.

Nothing like this could happen in the USA during the 1950s, just because government Hierarchy had little if any saying in what plant, when, and where, so Americans never experienced breadlines. However, the next 60 years brought in the tremendous growth of Hierarchy in America. Now individuals at the top of the Hierarchy of Federal Government do have a lot more power to dictate, for example, which sources of electric power to use: unreliable and expensive wind and solar instead of reliable and inexpensive nuclear and fossil fuels. And, since one is not buying electricity in stores, there will be no electricity lines. Still, people in America have already started experiencing rolling blackouts and will have to see more of this. As in the good old times of the USSR, propaganda media will promote false narratives supporting Hierarchy, and it will take some time for feedback to come through. But rest assured that at any point, individuals at the top will not experience any hardship caused by their decisions, and therefore it will take quite a bit of time for them to change the course. Another example would be the COVID pandemic that nicely demonstrated inadequacies of the Hierarchy method.

Conclusion

The most obvious and often unappreciated fact is that only humans think, feel, and act. The abstract entities such as governments do no such thing. Consequently, society's effective or not functioning depends on using a mix of the Hierarchy and Ownership methods of interaction and cooperation between humans in proportions most appropriate for a given level of technological and cultural development.

This mixing of methods makes every individual simultaneously belonging to some static structure of human relations such as family/business or government organization/locality/nation/state as a member and being a node in some flexible network of friends, colleagues, ideological, business, and cultural associates. In both cases: occupying a cell of a Hierarchical structure and being a node in a flexible network makes individuals play various roles appropriate for each method, sometimes sequentially but sometimes simultaneously.

The Hierarchy method features a duality of roles: every individual is both superior to someone and inferior to someone else at the same time. This duality makes the functioning of any group with multiple layers very complex and often inefficient because the demands of superiors and the needs of inferiors are often contradictory. Consequently, Hierarchy works well in uncomplicated cases - such situations as war or emergency, when the unity of goals makes it imperative to use some individuals as means to the ends of others. The Hierarchy is excellent in producing relatively simple goods like weapons when the only criteria are qualitative and quantitative superiority over enemy weapons. At the same time, any other parameters, whether esthetic, environmental or whatnot, are just insignificant. In the area of services Hierarchy method is the best in fighting an enemy when sacrificing individuals for the group is an expected norm. Another similar area where Hierarchy is great is implementing colossal construction projects, whether a vast irrigation system or the great wall or great temple, when demands for Human Capital are minimal and mainly in the form of manual efforts. The somewhat downside of Hierarchy is its dependency on the ideological allegiance of people to some abstractions as a basis of unity. As soon as the perception of the commonality of goals disappears, the individuals at lower levels of Hierarchy start pursuing separate objectives, which in the mild form leads to massive corruption and, in severe form, could explode and destroy society from inside.

The Ownership method is based on equality of roles for everybody, even if types and amounts of resources under the control of each individual are infinitely diverse. Therefore, this method is best for complex cases such as the functioning of the economy, cooperative development of a scientific project, etc. In such cases, individual objectives, inputs, and outputs are reconciled either via market prices for goods and services in the economy or cumulative accumulation of knowledge via a free exchange of information and cross-validation of experimental results and logical conclusions for scientific projects. On the other hand, the Ownership method of interactions does not work that well for war or emergency, except for a short time when all individuals voluntarily put themselves under somebody else's control.

Both methods of interaction, in reality, are always intertwined and could not possibly exist without each other in mass societies. No human being could maintain Ownership of one's own body, leave alone any other resources, against even a small group of people organized in Hierarchy because of the group's overwhelming superiority in physical power. This reality necessitates the existence of military and law enforcement Hierarchies. Correspondingly use of Hierarchy in business or science is necessary as long as it requires unchallenged coordination of activities of a group of people to pursue a relatively simple objective. However, it is impossible to use resources efficiently and effectively from higher levels of Hierarchy unless people at lower levels, who are in physical control over resources, supportive and enthusiastically comply with directives. To put it simply: a slave in chains could not possibly be the most efficient producer because of chains, whether chains are physical and made of iron or psychological and made of ideology and political correctness. Consequently, the effective use of Human Capital requires voluntary exchange and cooperation that only the Ownership method could support.

Part II. The Challenge of Human Redundancy and Suggested Solution

The Challenge of the Human Redundancy for Production

Development of the Challenge

For the initial long period of our species existence, humans obtained resources they needed directly from the environment by hunting and gathering. Like their close relatives - chimpanzees, humans also used war to push neighbors from some territory they coveted so they could grow their tribe at the expense of others. The big brain allowed humans to adjust to just about any climate condition, with weather ranging from freezing to sweltering, so they populated the whole planet, in the process, killing out or merging with all other humanoids. Humans also eliminated many different species that caused inconveniences for humans, like Saber Tooth Tigers, which liked to have humans for dinner, or Mammoths that probably provided too many dinners for humans. In addition, many other species disappeared when humans destroyed their habitat, often without even noticing this. Based on what we know from archeology and anthropology about hunter-gatherers, the informal Ownership method of interaction and cooperation was dominant during this time. People owned themselves and whatever staff they could carry on.

To the extent it was used, the Hierarchy was also mainly informal, flexible, and founded more on traditions and propensity of individuals to demonstrate superior abilities rather than on coercion and violence. Thus, I think it would be fair to say that it was a period of Ownership dominance over Hierarchy, even if there was no formal recognition of property and no formal Hierarchical order.

The next step in developing resource acquisition methods was the invention some 10,000 years ago of agriculture that allowed humans to produce many more resources such as food from the same territory than it would be possible to obtain via hunting and gathering. Agriculture, however, meant either settlement on one site needed to harvest results of work invested into planting and growing or accumulate herds of cattle that required effort to move this herd from one pasture to another and protect it from predators. In either case, it led to resource concentration in one place that made war and raiding a much more effective method of resource acquisition than anything else before.

The Hierarchy is a more effective way to implement such activities as warfighting, so it became the dominant method of human interaction and cooperation, giving humans great kings, supreme leaders, general secretaries, gods on earth, and other less than pleasant staff. However, Hierarchy has its limitations because it is a pretty lousy method of handling resources productively. Whether deciding what, when, and where to plant, maintain, and harvest, or to which pasture to move cattle and how best protect it, or a zillion other very complex activities, people have to do their best both physically and mentally to make it happen – an impossibility for inferiors under control of others. Moreover, while an overseer could somewhat control physical activity with a whip, he could not control the cognitive activity of others. So, even individuals in chains can think freely and regulate the level of their effort, despite the fear that expression of this thinking would be punished.

Consequently, as soon as a king and his band captured more than could be technically controlled from the top, the control had to be distributed down to the lower levels of Hierarchy. Moreover, because communication and information processing are always imperfect, they had to use formal or, more often, informal Ownership. These circumstances gave us the structure of society that lasted until recently with some king or great leader at the top, several layers of Aristocracy and Bureaucracy below controlling some subset of resources, either territorial or functional. The vast number of people that did the bulk of manual and cognitive work was at the bottom: either slaves, who did not own their bodies, or workers, who did have formal ownership of their bodies but not enough resources to feed these bodies, so they had to comply with directives of others. There also were people controlling small amounts of resources in various forms, which they could use to sustain themselves without being under the direct control of others, albeit under the constant threat of being robbed.

For a long time, such a relatively stable system maintained a dynamic equilibrium between production and robbery. However, in the last few centuries, the system grew more unstable, at least in some parts of the world. This development was a logical consequence of constant military competition between different Hierarchies, which usually ended with Hierarchy with better weapons and organization winning, albeit only temporarily until some other Hierarchy got ahead. The trick is that for members of the Hierarchy to have better weapons and organization, the people who produce weapons and manage organizations should do their best, which means expansion of Ownership of their bodies, minds, tools, and products. Such development leads to the growth of prosperity and improvement in technology, but at the cost of growing frustration of individuals at the higher levels of the Hierarchy, whose power decreases. Typically, members of the Hierarchy would respond by using their power to limit Ownership. Although these limitations provide for a short period of enjoying increased power over others, they would find out that productivity and, therefore, competitiveness, including militarily, of their society, had decreased.

The contradiction of the need to respect Ownership to be an effective bandit caused general systemic instability when different societies experimented with varying forms of relationship between these two methods of interaction and cooperation under evolutionary pressure that eliminates less effective community. Overall, this process led to technological progress that increased productivity as a decisive factor in the ability to mobilize resources and apply them to improve the military fitness of society.

This very long and ongoing process of technological progress produced increased returns on human effort in the form of goods and services. It has now arrived at the point when the productive activities of a tiny share of the population are sufficient to provide enough of everything for everybody. It is obviously at the level of needs, meaning functionality of an object, rather than non-functional features: for example, bag vs. brand name bag.

This remarkable course of events led to the crises of resource allocation because it left lots of individuals, which did not have Ownership of anything else but Human Manual Capital, **redundant.** That meant that nobody would transfer sufficient resources to redundant humans who have nothing to offer in exchange and are not a part of any Hierarchy. This redundancy caused riots, mass criminality, Luddite, and later socialist and communist movements and revolutions. The response was the increase in charity and expansion of internal activity of various Hierarchies directed at the development of welfare in the form of inclusion of redundant for production population into lowest levels of Hierarchy, with the correspondingly low level of resource allocation. It also included measures to increase the value of Human Cognitive Capital via education and allow unions to increase the competitiveness of individuals with low levels of Human Capital by monopolizing parts of the labor market.

These efforts eventually created a new type of relative stability of Welfare states by the second half of the XXth century. In this new set of conditions, most people could obtain education and, with it, some Human Cognitive Capital to produce goods and services that other people need. Another option that education provided was a place in some government or corporate Hierarchy where credentialed people either produced something that nobody needed or even did not produce anything. In either case, they would still get some resource allocation from the top in proportion to their place in the Hierarchy. Overall, the majority of people could obtain sufficient amounts of resources to be at least minimally satisfied.

Let's now look at where we are now in handling the challenge of continuously increasing productivity and consequently Human redundancy in more detail.

Current Handling of the Challenge of Human Redundancy

The current process combines the Ownership method of human interaction and cooperation with the Hierarchy method. The former applied to creating new resources necessary for consumption and future production. The latter used to control people and move most of the newly produced resources under the control of individuals at the top of multiple Hierarchies to distribute these resources down to individuals at lower levels of Hierarchies.

Here is the logic of the current process:

Individuals in control of Material Capital, either formal or informal Owners, interact with Owners of Human Capital via the employment process, creating new resources. However, individuals at the top of violent Hierarchies of governments limit these interactions by imposing various laws and regulations. They also get the first claim on produced resources via taxes. Then Owners of Material and Human Capital distribute the claims on the leftovers of the newly created goods and services between themselves according to market rates of return on various types of capital. The business profits, salaries, and benefits are representations of these claims. The Individuals at the top of corporate hierarchies retain a disproportionally high percentage of claims and share it with others in control of various corporate or government Hierarchies. This process occurs using multiple methods such as super-high salaries, stock options, bonuses, charitable donations, consulting fees to former government bureaucrats and politicians, and whatnot. Then they allocate some share of claims on resources to lower levels of corresponding Hierarchies who produce either nothing or inferior products and services, mostly regardless of market rates of return on Human Capital.

There is a continuum of Hierarchies that implement this logic in reality. Some are productive businesses of various sizes with mixed functionality of coordinating activities of Owners of Human or Material Capital to produce goods and services and capture a share of returns for redistribution from the top down. The others are just various governments and "Non-profit" organizations designed to capture resources produced elsewhere.

This continuum starts with those organizations where the primary method of resource acquisition for their members is a return on applied Capital, either Human or Material, and extends to those for which the preeminent way is Hierarchical allocation. Generally, the size of the business could be a good proxy for estimating the balance of Ownership vs. Hierarchy. Small businesses with less than 10-20 people could hardly afford to allocate resources via Hierarchy except on a small scale. Thus, for example, something like the proverbial "good for nothing boss's son in law" makes business less competitive because this person's salary should be covered either by higher prices for goods and services produced or underpayment to other employees. On the other hand, medium-sized businesses have more space for the Hierarchical method and more than a few Individuals who bring in less in Human Capital than they take out in claims. Finally, large businesses often are minimally productive and would be out of business if not protection provided by government Hierarchies via regulations, contracting, and other tools. There are also "Non-profit" Hierarchies, whose main aim is to coordinate corruption between government and private business individuals. They do it by excluding a significant share of the claims on resources from taxation and providing resource flow to well-connected individuals who are, at the moment, out of place in other Hierarchies.

The claims for resources have two primary forms:

- Money that allows resources acquisition on the open market, which means the best quality of resources available for the same quantity of money
- Benefits that allow resource acquisition within restrictions imposed by benefits providers. These resources are usually of lower quality because Individuals who decide on benefits always try to do it as cheaply as possible. However, if these are their benefits, they use different rules that allow the acquisition of goods and services of higher quality, sometimes even better than available for the money.

After obtaining claim on resources, Individuals exchange these claims for actual goods and services, which is not always easy, whether claims are in the form of money or benefits:

- In the case of money, the exchange of claims for goods and services occurs directly between two sides of the transaction, each trying to promote its interest. However, the ability to convert them into goods and services is regularly restricted by Individuals in control of the most potent Hierarchy – the government. Typically, these Individuals use authority over the money supply to increase this supply to satisfy claims of the members of the Hierarchy that do not produce anything of value. This increase in money generates inflation that could be general or partial. It could impact only some products and services, for example, housing and stock markets. It is even possible to hide it within the expansion of global trade, as it happens in the case of the USA when the perceived quality of the American dollar causes people around the world to exchange tangible goods and services for inflated dollar assets such as mortgage-based securities or even colored paper with a dollar sign on it.
- In the case of benefits, it is even funnier. The exchange occurs via an intermediary with interests at least partially different from both sides: benefits provider and recipient. For example, the provision of "free" education via some government Hierarchy mainly serves the interests of Individuals within this Hierarchy. This "free" education also quickly becomes indoctrination, helping politicians at the top by conditioning the population to support whatever political organization puts them at the top. For individuals at lower levels of such educational Hierarchy, it allows obtaining resources via hierarchical allocations at the level that they would never be able to get via free market of educational services.

This intermediary interest is the only reason for "benefits" methods. Looking at history, it is pretty apparent that benefits always come into play when there is a Hierarchy. Whether it is a minuscule Hierarchy of a small town, which leaders decided to tax the population to pay for a small school with one teacher or a vast socialist state that provides "free" healthcare and education, the key is that it is leaders of town or socialist state who decide what kind, quantity, and quality of services provided, not people who consume these services and pay for them via tax. The results are simple: the small-town teacher would keep telling students how great are the leaders of the small town and how much they should respect and admire them, or this teacher would have to find another job regardless of the education that kids are getting or not getting. Similarly, the "educators" of a socialist state with "free" education can forbid reading some books and force extensive studying of others, as well as providers of the "free" healthcare, could limit access to expensive treatments. Obviously, none of the limitations would apply to themselves and their families.

The Expansion of the Challenge of Human Redundancy

This arrangement worked relatively well when numbers of mixed (Material & Human) Capital Owners such as small business owners, professionals, specialists, skilled laborers, and others represented the vast majority of the population. However, with the progress of technology, it becomes less and less viable. Initially, the depreciation of Human Manual Capital by mass production and assembly lines had pushed the majority of the population away from independent production into the corporate world. Consequently, the corporations now produce most material goods using some hierarchical structures. As a result, only a small share at the bottom participates in making goods and services using their Human Manual Capital; meanwhile, the majority uses their Human Cognitive Capital.

Furthermore, the Information revolution extended the devaluation process to the Human Cognitive Capital. This process forced its owners to seek a place in the corporate Hierarchy where allocation of resources to their position compensates for the decrease in needs for their Human Cognitive Capital, making such individuals more dependent on their place in Hierarchy. Thus, we can now observe how the Information revolution, which started in the second part of the XX century, is increasingly doing to Human Cognitive Capital the same as the Industrial revolution did to Human Manual Capital. It makes Owners of such Human Capital **redundant** for producing goods and services.

The government Hierarchy also set up arrangements designed to conceal the true character of resources creation and allocation via regulations. Thus, for example, quite a few small businesses are created as attachments to big Hierarchies, either government or corporations. These businesses do not produce anything valuable but serve as tools to allocate resources obtained via taxes, regulation, national debt, or monopolistic surplus to well-connected individuals.

The challenge we are now facing is much more significant than before. Back then, society successfully handled the redundancy of Human Manual Capital via a combination of education to expand the Human Cognitive Capital of active and capable individuals and the welfare state to provide for passive and less capable. However, the challenge now comes from the low availability of places for competent individuals to be real actors rather than just passive recipients of allocated resources deprived of an opportunity for meaningful actions under self-control. This situation would guarantee the growth of unhappiness and frustration. Eventually, this frustration will find its way out, leading to conflict between individuals at the top and bottom of Hierarchies, with a possible explosive restructuring of societies similar to those in XVIII-XX centuries due to the growing redundancy of Human Manual Capital.

Potential Developments: Fork in the Road

There are two potential developments in the complex world of a massive and globally integrated economy: one based on the enormous dominance of the Hierarchy method and another based on the supremacy of the Ownership method.

One example of the former development implemented in real life by the Chinese communist party seemingly demonstrates the superiority of Chinese overwhelmingly Hierarchical Society comparatively to American Society with the much weaker authority of Hierarchy and much more prominent presence of Ownership. However, I think this perception of the Hierarchy's superiority is illusory because the Chinese Communist Party managed to obtain rapid development via massive foreign investment and transfer of technology and production to China in search of cheap labor and protection from environmental and other regulations. Another part of the illusion resulted from the strict control over information, which suppresses anything negative about the Chinese model and promotes a positive image. The Chinese communist party implements this control with the strong support of masses of western "intellectuals" who enjoy a high level of resources allocated to their places in various Hierarchies due to their credentials and connections rather than to their possession of marketable Human Cognitive Capital. Therefore, it is pretty reasonable for such "intellectuals" to promote everything supporting Hierarchy as the best way of social organization, whether in the current Chinese or historical Soviet incarnation.

Ownership dominance would reliably provide a high quality of goods and services, but it has many disadvantages, as demonstrated by the American way. For people who own nothing, or next to nothing, the perception of poverty and powerlessness is real psychological hardship, even if one is provided with goods and services that rich people of 100 years ago or contemporary members of fully

Hierarchical societies could not even imagine. These disadvantages of society with relatively strong Ownership are also greatly exaggerated by "intellectuals." The reality is that these disadvantages are caused not by the dominance of the Ownership method but the limitation of ownership to only the second and third components of the production process: Human and Material capital. Consequently, people with minimal Human Capital could not obtain psychologically sufficient amounts of goods and services within such limited Ownership. They had to rely on Hierarchical handouts, providing political support to restrictions of the Ownership method, which resulted in economic stagnation despite tremendous technological progress.

All above is valid only until Human Capital is the necessary part of the production process, but many things will change when machinery provides viable substitution. For example, the human individual initially pressed by the implementation of machines such as conveyor line to the limit of physical endurance and therefore prone to strike or rebellion is not required anymore – machines generally do better work and never rebel. Similarly, human individuals that used to be typing text or drawing blueprints according to directions of writer or engineer are not needed anymore. A writer can say what he wants for a computer to write, and an engineer would use drawing software rather than explaining what he needs in this blueprint to the technician. The next step would be AI producing a novel based on some vague direction of the potential reader or generating digital instructions for automatically creating whatever engineering product is required. Since Human nature and behavior define pluses and minuses of both Hierarchy and Ownership methods of interaction and cooperation, the removal of humans from the production process means that both approaches could be good enough for satisfying the physiological needs of humans. But it would be a different story for the psychological domain, which condition depends on the dominance of one method over another:

The Dominance of Hierarchy would mean that source of psychological satisfaction for people had to be adjusted to knowing their place and living by the rule: **"Kiss up Kick down"** with the availability of resources defined by superiors in a Hierarchy. The individuals at the top of the Hierarchy would decide the amounts and types of goods and services produced according to their needs, psychological and physiological, often in ways detrimental to individuals at the bottom.

The Dominance of Ownership, providing it deliver sufficient resources for everybody, would mean psychological satisfaction via a lifestyle of **"Freedom with Resources"** with the availability of new resources defined by free and effective use of existing resources that one already owns and successful cooperation with others. The amounts and types of goods and services produced would be decided by all individuals, including those at the lowest levels of income, according to their needs and reconciled via free-market covering everything, including environmental impact.

Suggested Way of Handling the Challenge

The Emerging Challenge of Human redundancy for producing goods and services has to be handled in a non-trivial way. Therefore, I suggest a response to the Emerging Challenge based on recognizing the importance of the first component of the production process, which until now was not explicitly recognized even if everybody uses it, and establishing **a payment process for this usage**. As noted at the beginning of this essay, this component is the **Common Inheritance** of humanity created in the past by mainly unknown individuals, constantly updated by mostly unknown individuals, which, therefore, equally belongs to all. This **Common inheritance**, with all its attributes: language, norms of behavior/interactions between people, and the multitude of know-hows, which are not subject to formal intellectual property rights, is the foundation not only for the production process but also for the human existence itself. Thus, for example, the vast majority of individuals sell their services based on the **Common Inheritance** in exchange for returns in proportion to the value of their services. Similarly, machines produce goods and services inevitably based on the **Common Inheritance**. However, whether it is human labor or devices controlled by AI, in either case, the **Common Inheritance** is decisive factor of production currently not accounted for and correspondingly not paid for.

The new process would assign equal property rights for the COMMON INHERITANCE as an <u>unalienable asset to all individuals while</u> providing a mechanism to obtain acceptable returns on this new type of asset.

Such returns would be no different than returns on any other asset commonly owned by several individuals and actively used by one. For example, let's assume that two siblings inherited a farm on condition always to maintain equal shares, with the only one sibling continuing farming. Meanwhile, another sibling moved to a city. One would reasonably expect the farmer to pay something to the city dweller to use his half of the property on the farm. This "something" would have variable amounts depending not that much on the farmer's performance as on the rental value of this farm. If the farming sibling is good and does better than average, it would be only fair if he keeps a proportionally higher share of the total returns. However, if a farming sibling does a lousy job, it would be reasonable if the city dweller still gets close to half of the average market rent on a similar farm as an asset.

Process of providing returns on COMMON INHERITANCE assets

It could work similarly to siblings' example. The people can establish equal rights to **Common Inheritance** as an asset equally belonging to all and allocated to everybody as time-dependent tradable securities – the equivalent of issuing securities in proportion to the rental value of our farm for a year divided 50-50 between our siblings. Since only one of our siblings uses the farm, this sibling would have to periodically buy another 50% of the rights to use this farm from a non-user.

Such arrangement would include a massive expansion of the Ownership method. All members of society could trade in shares of **Common Inheritance** between them, creating resource flow between individuals with direct control over other tangible or intangible resources (Material Capital and Human Capital) and individuals in possession of minimal to none productive resources or abilities.

Functionally it would be pretty feasible to set up. For example, the Hierarchy in control (state) could issue securities (let's call them **Common Inheritance Shares:** *CI-Shares* for short)* and then establish a process for using these *CI-Shares* to assure good returns for all. Here is how such a process could work:

1. Identify quantity and issue *CI-Shares* based on the totality of Material and Human Capital expressed as a share of the estimated Assets and the entirety of Income of all Individuals with corporate Assets and Income passed through to human owners of corporations. It could mean the issue of one unit of *CI-Shares* for every Monetary Unit of Wealth and Income reported.
2. Allocate these securities (*CI-Shares*) equally and periodically to all individuals
3. Create incentives for all to trade these *CI-Shares* for money to equalize coverage of Individual wealth and income by these *CI-Shares*. These incentives would be nothing more than protecting property rights by assuring payments for the use of indivisible assets equally owned by all individuals.

The total amount of *CI-Shares* issued for a period should equal the total *CI-Shares* allocated. Since this amount is linked to accumulated wealth and generated income, the legislature would determine the INHERITANCE RATE that regulates the ratio between accumulated wealth and current human effort as sources of the new resources. Therefore, it would prevent somebody with sufficient wealth and low income from avoiding payment for **Common Inheritance**. One can use a simple formula defining requirement/allocation for each individual.

INDIVIDUAL REQUIREMENT/ALLOCATION for *CI-Shares*:

Number of CI-Shares = ASSETS * INHERITANCE RATE + INCOME FROM ALL SOURCES

As in any exchange with the **Ownership** method, the price of *CI-Shares* would be variable and dependent on usual market variables: timing, estimates of the current and future values, and so on. The total amount of resource transfers via this process would depend on the productive abilities of owners of tangible assets and earners of income compared to others. If we apply this process to a population with approximately equal productivity levels – for example, a society of self-sufficient farmers, then the amount of resource transfer would be negligible. However, if we apply it to a community in which AI-controlled machines massively substitute human productive efforts, with just a few humans owning these tools, then the transfer would be massive. In contemporary society, when a significant minority of the population are still productive owners of capital and earners of income, the transfer levels would be somewhere in the middle between these two extremes.

The process would be predicated on the apparent reality that some owners and earners are more productive than average or possess more than average tangible assets. Therefore, the average amount of *CI-Shares* allocated to them would not be sufficient to match their requirements for these *CI-Shares*. In this case, they would have to cover the difference by buying additional *CI-Shares*. On the other side of the equation, individuals with materially lower productivity levels or property would have excessive amounts of *CI-Shares* allocated to them, creating the opportunity to sell these excessive *CI-Shares*.

These securities could be periodically redeemable by the Treasury as a last resort. The price for the average number of *CI-Shares*, in this case, should be sufficient to support minimally acceptable levels of resource availability for individuals without assets or income if they cannot sell their allocation of *CI-Shares*. In contrast, individuals with assets or income above average who are not willing or unable to buy a sufficient number of *CI-Shares* on the market to cover their requirement would have to buy it from Treasury at prices materially higher than market prices. Such arrangement would mean protecting property rights in **Common Inheritance** for unproductive individuals with next to nothing personal net worth. It would also mean enforcement of rent payments against productive or wealthy delinquent individuals who are unwilling to pay for the use of valuable assets they only partially own.

If the wealthy and productive decide to participate, they would have much more control over amounts and forms of payments. The probable outcome would be a massive effort by such wealthy and productive individuals to educate poor and unproductive individuals in preference of selling their *CI-Shares* over getting the minimum. As always with humans, one could expect that unpredictability of the Ownership Method of exchange and cooperation would create inequality of results, with some people buying/selling their CI-Shares at higher/lower prices. Still, it would be an excellent stimulus to improve market performance.

Unlike various welfare schemas or universal guaranteed income (UBI), this method treats people as humans. It provides them with plenty of space to act, haggle, and improve, rather than treating them as animals that had to be supplied with food, water, shelter, or money and deprived of free will and ability to act.

Assuming INHERITANCE RATE 5%:

- Individual **AA** has Assets Worth $10,000,000 and is highly productive, generating $500,000 in income. It would mean that this individual's requirement for *CI-Shares* is: 10,000,000 * 0.05 + 500,000 = **1,000,000 *CI-Shares***

- Individual ***BB is average among population***, having Assets Worth $200,000 and $40,000 in income, meaning individual requirement:

  200,000*0.05 + 40,000 = **50,000 *CI-Shares***

- Individual **CC** is not productive at all and has no assets or income whatsoever, so the requirement is 0 ***CI-Shares***

Since the average amount is 50,000, **Treasury** would issue 50,000 *CI-Shares* valid for one year to each of these people, so:

AA would have to buy 1,000,000-50,000= 950,000 *CI-Shares,*
BB would have nothing to sell or buy
CC would have 50,000 *CI-Shares* to sell.

The price would be variable depending on the market. For example, let's assume it was $0.2 per *CI-Share* when **AA** and **CC** decided to complete the transaction, so: **CC** would sell his allocation of 50,000 *CI-Shares* for $10,000 to **AA,** which would place **CC** into the 10% percentile of USA income distribution in 2020.

After this transaction, **AA** would still need to buy an additional 900,000 CI-Shares from others like **CC** or pay tax to Treasury at whatever the legislature defined as the correct rate sufficiently above the market. Depending on how good buyer **AA** is, it could be more or less than the tax in the current arrangement. However, the difference with the current setup is enormous because now **AA** has some interest in increasing the productive abilities of **CC.** Correspondingly, **CC** becomes a market participant striving to improve selling skills instead of being the passive recipient of loot. Thus, it would inevitably make this person potentially more productive.

Another probability is that **CC** could find a better deal, so somebody pays $0.3 for half of the allocation, making **CC** better off by (25,000*0.3+25,000*0.2) − (50,000*0.2) = $2,500 and forcing **AA** to find another seller for this 25,000 *CI-Shares.*

Finally, the massive benefit for everybody would be the elimination of the need for a vast redistributive Hierarchy that currently uses force to extract resources from **AA** and **BB** under the pretense of helping **BB** and **CC,** while in reality retaining most of it to satisfy their own physiological and psychological needs and wants.

Expected Net Results of the New Arrangement

So, let's see what the intended consequences are:

- Individual **AA** now has no incentive to lobby Hierarchy (Government) to decrease taxes used for wealth redistribution or provide loopholes but is motivated to invest some time, effort, and even money to make **CC** more productive. **AA** may or may not succeed, but this action would make sense, especially if a partnership lasts for a few years.

- Individual **CC** would cease being a passive recipient of resources because active participation could bring better results immediately, not sometime in the future.

- Another significant change would also occur in the relationship between **AA** and **CC,** currently ranging from non-existent to hostile. By making **CC** more productive, **AA** would better understand **CC's** problems and challenges and consequently would have better chances to help, adding intangible psychological benefit to the mix. Indeed, **AA** would have another couple of dozen **CC**s to deal with to cover his requirement. However, resourceful and deeply incentivized **AA** would do much better than some government bureaucrats whose choice is to keep people poor or lose the job of providing them with welfare if they cease to be poor. It is also possible that human-to-human interaction would decrease **CC**'s resentment toward more successful **AA** and the contempt that the hard-working **AA** feels toward "takers."

- Even if, at first glance, individual **BB** should be indifferent to the whole thing, it is not so. Nobody is perfectly average, so **BB** would have something to sell one year and buy another. This arrangement could add stability to **BB's** situation allowing for more risk-taking and maybe more returns. Moreover, if **AA** and **CC** succeeded in making **CC** more productive, overall productivity would increase, benefiting everybody, **BB** included.

- Finally, another essential side effect would be a dramatic decrease in the number of individuals who depend on any Hierarchy. Independence from either government or corporations for resource allocation would increase the freedom of individuals to do what they like doing, rather than what they have to do to survive.

What happens if nobody needs to work for a living

Let's now look at not so impossible future in which AI-controlled machines can do all the jobs.

For example, let us look at a genius writer who could use language with an incredible skill comparable to the greatest writers in history but generates little income because only a few highly educated people read his works. At the same time, many readers prefer pulp fiction produced by a famous writer and written in the most primitive form imaginable. The current model forces the genius writer to get the support of a politician who uses taxes to finance the activity of our genius with no regard to the wishes of people who pay these taxes.

If my suggestion applied, all these taxpayers would be off the hook, and only high-income individuals, including the prosperous pulp fiction writer, would have to buy *CI-Shares* from our genius. This way, the genius would have sufficient proceeds from sales of *CI-Shares* to be free writing masterpieces full time. With the advance of Artificial Intelligence (AI), it is easy to imagine that the production of pulp fiction switched to automated mode. After some adjustment period, it would produce a billionaire or two out of original creators of AI tools. After that, everybody could have a personal AI writer producing entertainment fiction adjusted exactly to this consumer's current state of mind as recognized via reading brain waves. Then we would have no human producers of pulp fiction, just these couple of billionaires with property rights over AI tools.

Consequently, these billionaires would have to buy *CI-Shares* from "everybody else," including our genius and former pulp fiction writer. But, who knows, maybe free from needs to make a living, many people become more educated and interested in masterpieces. In this case, the demand for writings of our genius skyrocketed because his writing significantly improved after liberation from the need to satisfy politicians' preferences. The result could be that our genius makes so much income that he would have to buy *CI-Shares* from the former pulp fiction king rather than depend on the government handouts.

The Implementation

What to do

Historically, significant societal changes occur via massive and often bloody upheavals such as conquests, revolutions, and civil wars. American nearly unique written and somewhat respected Constitution combined with regular and relatively fair elections created the opportunity for massive changes without such upheavals. It is a generally slow and complex process that requires understanding and support for the changes among the majority of the active population. However, it is achievable by creating a movement with a simple and clear objective expressed in the form of the Constitutional Amendment.

Over nearly 250 years of American history, such significant changes occurred multiple times, with only one of such changes applied via the massive and bloody Civil

War. However, even in this case, it was not the civil war within one polity but rather a war between two coalitions of multiple polities.

Here are examples of such massive changes and/or failed attempts:

1789-1791 Original Bill of Rights (Amendments 1 - 10) explicitly recognizing individual rights and establishing limitations on government power, at least at the Federal level.

1865-1870 Elimination of Slavery and Constitutional Racism (Amendments 13 - 15) took more than 100 years of on-and-off struggles to incorporate into the culture.

1913 Transfer from the Union of States into the Federal Republic (Amendments 16-17) initiating more than 100 years of ongoing takeover of the control over the country by the Federal Hierarchy.

1918-1932 Failed attempt of a massive cultural transfer away from the use of alcohol (Amendment 18 rejected by 21)

Correspondingly the significant change that I suggest could and should be implemented via the Constitutional Amendment, which would require a prolonged period of education, discussions, and political fight to obtain sufficient support of the majority of the active population. I want to suggest the following definition within the genre of constitutional amendments:

> **1   We recognize that everything that constitutes Common Inheritance of the people of the United States, such as language, norms of behavior, and general know-how, is the necessary component of any productive activities that generate wealth and income. This Common Inheritance equally belongs to all citizens. Therefore, the individuals who use it effectively should provide compensation for this use to individuals who fail to do it.**
>
> **2   Such compensation will be supported by issuing quantifiable Common Inheritance Securities for such rights to all individuals equally, with the requirement for individuals whose wealth and income exceed average allocation to buy these securities to cover such excess combined with the option for individuals whose wealth and income are below average to sell such securities**
>
> **3   All transactions in Common Inheritance securities should occur within one year of their issue between individuals and be registered as such.**
>
> **4   Individuals in possession of Common Inheritance Securities over their wealth and income who fail to sell them at market price will have the option to trade them into Treasury at a price defined by Congress at the**

The critical question is who would be interested in implementing such an amendment and who would be interested in preventing this from happening.

Individuals who would fight for or against it

Humans' nature, as it is, has a substantial prejudice against losing anything, especially if this anything is the foundation of their wellbeing. However, with the advance of AI and increasing redundancy of Human Cognitive Capital, it will probably be individuals in possession of such capital or in the process of acquiring it who would discover that its massive devaluation hurt them and start fighting for a change.

This process is already ongoing since the early 1990s when increasing computerization of information processing pushed out of job lots of people in possession of such capital: middle managers, travel agents, all kinds of small businesses that transferred wholesale trade into retail, and so on. Some, probably even majority, of these individuals succeeded in either rebuilding their Human Capital within some new niche or relatively smoothly moved to lower levels of some corporate or government Hierarchy, eventually reaching somewhat comfortable retirement with the help of the stock market and real estate inflation pumped up by the massive government debt. But unfortunately, quite a few others failed, causing the rise in deaths of despair, decline of many rural small cities, and formerly great American industrial centers of 1950-the 60s.

The older generations of Americans, impacted by the increasing redundancy of their Human Capital during the first 30 years of this process, tried moving the country in various directions while avoiding radical change. The range was from Reagan's conservatism to Obama's non-totalitarian statism, but neither one could possibly work. Now it is the turn of younger generations who will increasingly recognize that there is no place for their dream of independence and freedom based on their Human Cognitive Capital of high-tech skills. They are currently in the process of finding out that all they can get is either a low-level place in some Hierarchy or just a place in some low-income shelter playing games and living on some type of Universal Basic Income. In either case, educated and credentialed individuals will not be happy because meaningless jobs combined with a constant fear of superiors in Hierarchy could not possibly satisfy their needs for a meaningful life. At the same time, uncredentialed could very well find miserable welfare existence intolerable, even if basic biological needs are satisfied. Let's assume that these two types of individuals recognize that they own a share of asset of great value – Common Inheritance, which others use without providing them with any compensation whatsoever. In that case, they could become active in implementing changes that would give them market-defined fair compensation for using their share.

Some individuals possessing significant material wealth or top places in some Hierarchy, especially the government, would resist such change since it would make them pay for something they get for free now. However, there will be relatively few such individuals because recognition of Common Inheritance as an asset does not deprive anybody of existing Human or Material Capital. It just increases the need to use it effectively. The only individuals that will be hurt are individuals in strong psychological need of power over others, obtainable only by getting a place at the top levels of Hierarchy. With the change of dominant method of interaction and cooperation from Hierarchy to Ownership, there will be fewer such places, correspondingly diminishing opportunities to exercise power over others. The only realistic chance for power-crazies to continue dominance of the Hierarchy method is the mass indoctrination of people in preference of Hierarchy over Ownership. This indoctrination somewhat works with the young but quickly wears out when the young encounter life's realities and find out what works and what does not. With massive depreciation of Human Capital, young individuals would grow up feeling surrounded and depressed by adults frustrated in their meaningless jobs and stressed by abuses from superiors in Hierarchy. In such an environment, indoctrination in Hierarchy's superiority over Ownership would be as effective as indoctrination in Socialism's superiority over Capitalism was in the late period of the Soviet Union.

Consequently, the search for alternatives will intensify. It would lead either to establishing the dominance of the Ownership method or to a sequence of Hierarchies periodically overthrowing each other by promising a more meaningful life. Such a series of Hierarchies could continue indefinitely if the Hierarchy's superiority paradigm continues uninterrupted.

Challenges to Common Inheritance Rights Suggestion
Here I hope to review some potential challenges for the suggested solution and analyze these challenges.

Common Inheritance is equally available to everybody. Therefore, it would be unfair to force the successful producers to buy shares from those who failed

The use of force to coerce more productive individuals to buy *CI-Shares* from less effective is nothing more and nothing less than enforcing property rights. It is not different from calling the police when one individual got into the car co-own with others and drove away without any agreement or compensation for co-owners. In both cases, somebody uses an object of value that belongs to others (s) without their agreement. Whether this object of value belongs as shared property to other family members or business partners or all citizens of the country or all humans currently living does not matter. What does matter is the fact of belonging that necessitates compensation for use. The established rules of the game define this fact of belonging. These rules currently recognize car ownership as a property of material conglomeration of metals, plastic, and an immaterial combination of specified intellectual property such as patents and brand name incorporated into this car. As soon as we recognize the currently undefined Common Inheritance such as language, manner of behavior, and a million other things as an intangible property that equally belongs to all, we'll acknowledge the need for compensation. Correspondingly, the fairness of such compensation enforcement becomes no different from the fairness of enforcing payment for a community car's personal use.

It would be anything from complex to impossible to collect accurate data on the use of Common Inheritance and define compensation

Actually, it would not, because there is no human activity whatsoever without using Common Inheritance; any difference in income or wealth, regardless of how measured, would include unequal use of something that belongs equally to all. So, the compensation would eliminate this inequality of productive use: those who use more, as defined by resulting wealth and income, would compensate those who use less. The *CI-Shares* issued per information from well-established tax systems could provide a basis for such compensation. The actual material value compensating for these "more and less" is just a perception of value in the minds of individuals and should be based not on some defined amount but rather on the results of tradeoffs within these minds expressed via market prices for *CI-Shares*.

It would take a little time before giant corporations start trading CI-Shares in bulk, eventually equalizing price at the level just above minimal. After that, it all would come down to another form of guaranteed income, only with additional profits for the intermediary.

The usual motivation for business is profit, and it would not be easy to achieve in this case because all transactions would occur between individuals and be registered as such. It means that all sides would know the transaction price, and it is hard to believe that individuals selling their *CI-Shares* would knowingly agree to get less than the stated amount or pay somebody extra for mediation. It is much more probable that some wealthy individuals who need lots of *CI-Shares* to cover their excessive wealth and income will need help because of the scale of transactions. However, these people are sophisticated enough to keep the cost of this help as low as possible, which would lead to competition and a variety of exchange prices that come with it. It is pretty easy, for example, to imagine an electronic auction for trading *CI-Shares* where the price includes some intangible benefit of selling *CI-Shares* to some entertainment or sports star.

The overall price of *CI-Shares*, as anything else, would be defined by supply and demand. Since the number of *CI-Shares* issued is proportional to average, the only way demand falls below supply is when individuals with wealth and income above average would refuse to buy *CI-Shares* on the market. In this case, they will force people dependent on this transaction to survive at the acceptable minimum level, but they will do it at the price of high levels of taxation.

It would probably work the other way around – the demand to be higher than supply. A significant part of the population with wealth and income just slightly below average could decide that it is not worth participating in the *CI-Shares* market and prefer redeeming their shares at the minimum from the Treasury or even wholly neglecting it. In this case, the price will go up. Wealthy individuals would apply some effort to convince everybody with an excess of *CI-Shares* to participate in the exchange. They could do it either via advertising or by providing some benefits on top of the transaction price. In either case, as long as the market price for *CI-Shares* plus transaction cost is below the government's tax on failure to cover excessive income or wealth with *CI-Shares*, it makes more sense to buy CI-Shares than pay tax.

If prices of CI-Shares start getting too high, non-productive individuals with no property would be getting nearly the identical amounts of resources as productive, leaving the latter with no incentive to work.
This situation could happen if the production of the most goods and services becomes entirely automated, so practically all income from their sales goes to a few owners of Material Capital. Consequently, individuals without Material Capital would have so little wealth and income from their heavily depreciated Human Capital that they will entirely depend on *CI-Shares* for living. This dependency would put the whole process outside of the standard supply and demand model, moving it to the area of politics, in which a tax rate close to 100% is not something inconceivable. In this case, a few remaining productive individuals could potentially shut down their activity.

This scenario misses an essential point: there are multiple non-monetary benefits from being productive: self-esteem, prestige, satisfaction from achieving something, etc. True, many of these benefits depend on the indoctrination of individuals, but the evolutionary developed human need to be active is probably strong enough to prevent a majority of people from being idle. So whatever activities will be preferable, at least some of them generate income and create wealth above average and, consequently, keep the process going.

Even from the point of view of greed, complete cessation of productive activities is not feasible. It is because amounts of obtained income or accumulated wealth represent tremendous psychological value as the measure of success. Correspondingly, people will direct the greed more at getting a psychological value rather than something purely material. The need for top producers to buy *CI-Shares,* even at a high market price, in no way diminishes this psychological value as long as it is not destroyed by the feeling of being robbed, which is quite close to the sense of being taxed.

It would be impossible to define investors' real wealth because corporate securities' prices are fluid, and corporations own each other, creating complex networks of ownership that would be impossible to unwind and evaluate.

As much as corporations own each other, in the end, there are always human beings who own everything. These human beings are not necessarily wealthy business owners. They could be participants of some pension funds, owners of insurance policies, or owners of a few company securities. In the current environment, accountants routinely produce multiple financial data about corporations for governments and investors, so breaking information about their wealth and income to the individual investor's level would be quite possible. The amount of computer processing required to accomplish it would be well within boundaries of currently available computer power, even if it were impossible to achieve a decade or two ago. It would raise some exciting accounting issues related to the current value of corporations regardless of market valuation, but it should not be such a huge problem either. At the end of this process, an individual investor could use this information for reporting needed to estimate the number of *CI-Shares* based on the value of the investor's share of corporate assets and income rather than volatile stock market prices.

Part III. Relevant Parts of Underlying World View

Human Individuals

When one thinks about processes in human society, it is essential to keep in mind that there is one and only one type of thinking, feeling, and acting entities – human beings. Everything else that is treated as such, like state, government, corporation, and whatnot, that makes "collective" decisions and implements "collective" actions, are just abstractions that disguise the thinking and acting of individuals. We'll look in detail at how this "collective" staff works a bit later, but first and foremost, let's look at real thinkers and actors – individual human beings.

Here is my understanding: **Human is a self-directing entity capable to:**

- *Create, process, and retain information in the form of knowledge and skills*
- *Maintain this knowledge distributed between multiple individual human brains and external databases*
- *Consciously define objectives for the achievement of some conditions of living*
- *Act to achieve these objectives in cooperation with other humans by combining individual knowledge, skills, and actions into coordinated activity via words, sounds, images, smells, and other methods.*

Levels of Human existence

The table below represents the Levels of Human Existence from the bottom up and how they work together:

LEVELS AND RANGES OF HUMAN EXISTENCE					
MODIFIERS OF EXISTENCE					
Actions Availability Level	From **Inability** to Act to High Probability of **Success** of Action	*FREEDOM OR LACK THEREOF*			
		Agency as Ability to Act Independently		Availability of Resources Neccesary for Action	
Parameters of Existence Level	From **Suffering** from dissonance between Desired and Perceived Parameters to **Happiness** from Anticipation of and Satisfaction from achievement of Desired Parameters	*DESIRED Vs. PERCEIVED PARAMETERS:*			
		Health	Wealth	Interactions	Sex
ABSOLUTE NECESSITIES					
Meaning Level	From **Self-termination** to **Self-satisfaction**	Self-Confirmation: Prove of Believes in "Who Am I" and "My Place in Universe"			
Survivability Level:	Staying **Alive** or **Not**	Air (Minutes)	Water (Hours)	Sleep (Days)	Food (Weeks)

Figure 1. Matrix of Human Existence

Survivability Level.

This level relates to purely biological survival needs. If a human being fails to satisfy these needs, this human ceases to exist. This level is typical for all animals, albeit in different combinations.

Meaning Level

Human-specific parts of the brain support this purely human level. It relates to individuals' notion of self, place of self among other humans, and even within the universe. As soon as biological conditions of existence are satisfied, at least at the minimal level required for survival, the Meaning Level becomes the most crucial level of human existence. The needs of this level are infinitely diverse and depend on an individual's socialization and indoctrination into some religious or quasi-religious worldview, which begins at the moment of birth. Initially, a human accepts this worldview as given without question. After that, the human continuously develops various adjustments to the initial worldview via interactions with the environment, including other individuals, and internal physiological and psychological changes. The normal condition of this level is slight dissatisfaction with whatever status an individual believes to possess. Interestingly enough, in extreme situations, this human-specific level of meaning could override requirements of Survivability Level leading to self-sacrifice for a cause or suicide.

Parameters of Existence Level

This level represents parameters of human existence, which go way beyond necessities of Survivability and Meaning levels. It includes multiple areas of human life, which are in constant dynamic equilibrium between perceived and desired parameters of life when the variance between these parameters pushes humans to act to minimize this variance. The Parameters of existence provide specific details for an individual's life and put meat on the skeleton of Meaning, often changing it in the process.

Action Availability Level

This level defines what actions are available to a human, either to obtain necessities of Survivability and Meaning levels or to modify Parameters of Existence to decrease variance between Perceived and Desired Parameters. The technological and societal external conditions define the level of individual freedom available as the combination of personal agency that allows choosing a course of action and the availability of resources needed to implement this action. I want to illustrate this point with a real-life example:

a. A well-to-do professional in the USSR wanted to go on vacation to Western Europe. However, the Soviet government denied permission, stripping this individual of Freedom to use his Agency.
b. A few years later, as a legal immigrant to the USA, this professional could go anywhere in the world without any permission. However, the amount of money available was too small to go anywhere, so now, despite him having the Agency, the lack of Resources led to the same result: limitation on Freedom and no-go.
c. A few more years later, the same person, now a well-to-do professional in the USA, had Agency and Resources to go anywhere at will, meaning had Freedom with Resources.

Dynamics of existence

As with everything else with humans, dynamics are as critical as static. Whatever conditions a human is in, if it is changing in the direction of this human's desires, an individual is getting closer to happiness. Correspondingly, when it changes in the direction opposite to desired, humans get closer to unhappiness. The absolute level of parameters of existence above the level of survival usually would be individual specific and adjusted to, as long as the individual perceives them as acceptable or unavoidable. This dynamic nature of humans explains why winners of the lottery and sufferers of sudden disability restore their previous level of happiness just a few months after the life-changing event. However, when an individual finds some change in parameters unacceptable, for example, limitations on freedom where there was no such limitation before, then action could follow. It explains why revolutions happen not in societies at extreme levels of misery, even when people die from starvation, but rather in communities that experience sudden and fast deterioration of perceived parameters of existence. The explosion, however, becomes inevitable if enough active people are unhappy, even if the society stays way above survivability levels and nobody is starving.

Stages of existence

There is also an essential point to make, which is that humans go through various periods of life when their mental understanding of self and world develops through specific stages, leading to typical patterns of behavior:

The first stage is developing the human embryo into an individual capable of self-directing behavior. During this stage, an organism is physically growing, acquiring new abilities from walking to talking, and undergoing socialization. This process includes language acquisition, internalization of cultural patterns, and indoctrination into the dominant ideology of the individual's society.

The second stage occurs when an individual mainly completed physical formation, developed some understanding (usually only partially correct) of Self and Self's relation to others, and overall identified desired parameters of existence. After that, the individual leaves the environment where previous growing occurred and moves to the real world where the individual's ideals obtained from childhood and desirable levels of parameters of existence encounter reality. At this point, an individual has to reconcile the ideals with reality. One of the most curious features of this period is the typical initial rejection of the need for such reconciliation and an attempt to change the world to fit ideals. In society, which is in the condition of stability and general satisfaction with life by the majority of the people, this youthful rebellion quickly fizzles out, allowing the vast majority of youngsters to move on to the next stage. However, in a society, which is unstable, whether for reasons of war, economic instability, or whatever, this rebellion could become a fuse that would explode the existing world and dramatically change it. The latest several centuries provided multiple examples of this occurring, usually leading to tremendous suffering and violent deaths.

The third and last stage occurs when the individual reconciles Self, Desired, and Perceived parameters of existence to reality and starts acting to close the gap between Perceived and Desired within the framework of this reality. The dynamic looping process of evaluation-actions-reevaluation continues as long as this human exists. It does not mean that this process involves only marginal changes. On the contrary, some changes could be significant: A deeply religious person could become a militant atheist, the hustling businessman could become born again religious zealot, and idealistic Commie or Nazi could become cynical hustling businessmen. The range of changes is infinite, but one condition is true in nearly all cases: this is the process of Self-Indoctrination, which is very difficult if at all possible, to influence from outside.

INFERENCE: *The dynamic nature of human existence means that achieving some set of parameters of existence defined as happiness from the outset is impossible. The moment of achievement is the moment when Desired parameters change to some new and different set of Desired parameters, modifying an individual's understanding of happiness. For example, suppose an individual has enough resources and the ability to consistently move from one set of Perceived Parameters to the next, preferable one. In that case, his existence could be a happy state of the pursuit of happiness. On the other hand, the consistent inability to approach Desired Parameters would mean that an individual would be in a persistent state of unhappiness, resulting in hate directed at anybody and anything perceived to be causing this failure.*

In short, to keep humans happy and peaceful, one needs to assure realistic character of both Perceived and Desired Parameters and feasibility of resource acquisition for practical actions necessary for moving from former to latter.

Human Groups

Human life occurs in groups, so the typical individual's existence includes group participation, often in many groups simultaneously. Individuals belong to a group based on characteristics that could be intrinsic to individuals and unchangeable, such as genetic makeup, cultural background, and initial socialization. Alternatively, such attributes could be changeable: territorial, ideological, business, recreational, sports team affiliation, and so on – the variety is infinite.

When an individual belongs to a group, either inherently or at the moment, it defines the attitude and actions of this individual and the actions of others directed at him. It could be very complicated because individuals at the top who control the actions and behavior of group members could compete for resources within and without the group, so an individual who belongs simultaneously to the multitude of competing groups could have a pretty difficult time handling it.

As a result, all individuals have some hierarchy of groups in their minds. People constantly reshuffle this hierarchy depending on their Meaning of Existence changes and perceived **Parameters of Existence**. Moreover, the individuals in the group have different characteristics and priorities, which to a significant extent frame their actions that quite often could be conflicting: in support of one group that an individual belongs to, while in detriment to another group this individual also belongs. An excellent example from the XX century would be a communist son of a rural peasant family confiscating food in his village and condemning his own family to starvation. It happens because his **Meaning of Existence** was reformed by deep indoctrination into socialist ideals overwriting the initial **Meaning of Existence** as a member of this family.

Decision making in the group
Any decision is always the product of the individual mind and therefore limited by individual brain capacity, which typically considers only a few factors out of the multitude relevant for any particular decision. In reality, seemingly collective decisions and intellectual processing are either parallel processing that individuals reconcile via interaction or complex processing divided into various sub-decisions or both. Decisions in a small group of interacting individuals typically include the disproportional influence of some individuals over others. In the small group of peers, effective interaction would allow for a better decision quality by bringing to attention some factors known to one group member but not others. However, if the influence of one individual were overwhelming, the quality of decision would be highly dependent on the personal quality of this individual. The limited brain capacity leads to considering only a few factors and limit effective interaction to only a few people, making the quality of decisions highly dependent on group organization, especially for complex groups that include millions of individuals.

There are two main modes of decision-making in gigantic and complex groups. The first one is the division of the complex group into the multitude of small groups making decisions in their competence area, then acting and interacting via voluntary exchange of goods, services, and ideas when some subset of these decisions need reconciliation. The second mode is creating a hierarchical structure when decisions are made at the top and then pushed down to everybody else. The former model would provide for generally competent and effective decisions, while the latter would be a mixed bag of intelligent and incompetent decisions. The considerable difference between models in the quality of decisions results from the different quality of the feedback loop, not the consequence of the quality of individuals. The wrong decision in a small group would quickly deteriorate life parameters for members of this group, causing them to modify this decision rapidly. In a vast hierarchical group, the impact would be quick for individuals at the bottom but slow for individuals at the top who make decisions.

For example, a small business with a few partners will see an immediate decrease in revenues and profits, impacting the quality of life for its members if the decision is wrong. It would not be a case for a big corporation where it could be years before bad choices negatively impact the lives of the CEO and others at the top. It would be even less efficient for some socialized entity when the quality of decision never affects the quality of life of individuals at the top. Even super powerful Artificial Intelligence that considers all potential factors and all conceivable **Parameters of Existence** of all individuals while producing one decision for everybody could not remove these limitations. It is because gaps between **Perceived and Desired Parameters** are fluid and change all the time. It is not a problem when individuals make decisions for Self because responsibility for results resides with a decision-maker. It is a big problem when somebody makes decisions for others and forces them to comply. In this case, the unsatisfactory result leads to resentment against the decision-maker, which inevitably undermines the group's stability.

Actions of individuals in the group

Like decision-making, an individual's actions nearly always include interaction with other individuals who may or may not belong to the same group. These interactions come down in two forms: **Exchanging** goods and services and **Cooperating** in the synchronization of individual activities. In both cases, individuals could do it either voluntarily or under coercion. Since individuals always direct their activities to improve their **Parameters of Existence**, synchronization of desired parameters is essential for success. However, it is also highly dependent on individuals' **Meaning of Existence,** which could be the dominant factor in individuals' actions.

A simple, well-known, and compelling example would be an individual's behavior in the battle. In this case, there is an internal conflict between multiple desired parameters: survive, win this battle, maintain the respect of others, maintain self-respect, and so on. For example, a poorly trained soldier could quickly turn around and run, even if it is evident that such behavior dramatically decreases the probability of achieving desired parameters, including survival, because troops retreating in panic get massacred. On the other hand, a well-trained and experienced soldier would stand his ground even when survival chances are nil. In this case, even if survival were not an option anymore, keeping fighting and maintaining self-respect would be preferred parameters.

Interaction across the groups and complex groups

Another critical issue is the interaction between individuals belonging to different groups. The history of humanity resulted in the development of huge groups that include millions of individuals, each of which belongs to quite a few various groups: family, locality, nations, religion, race, ethnic background, economic class, language, profession, friendships, and whatever else imaginable. Correspondingly individuals act according to the perceived interest of whatever group is dominant in their mind at the time. Sometimes such actions result in a war, either cold or hot, when individuals in one group believe that they could not coexist with individuals aligned with the other group on current terms.

Historically these were the wars between nations for resources and territory or civil wars, either religious or racial or ideological, to homogenize the group. Generally desired outcome was the submission of members of one group to members of another, but in rare cases, it was the destruction of all members of the other group. Finally, after about 10,000 years of such wars, humanity developed weapons of self-annihilation and initiated the general intermixing of individuals via mass communications, travel, and migration across the globe. As a result, we now have complex multi-group societies that substituted wars by the struggle for supremacy within complex, multilayered groups, making internal stability generally more challenging than anything else.

Stability of complex group that includes a multitude of smaller groups

The key to the stability of a complex group is an effective hierarchy of groups it consists of, which somewhat paradoxically could be achieved only via tolerance when individuals in control apply group's mores variably with each level of the Hierarchy. The most flexible and broadest scope of the rules should be at the bottom. The higher up one moves, the range of the rules should decrease. For example, if we look at the simplified structure: family-locality-state, the most comprehensive scope of requirements and decision-making should be at the lowest level of the hierarchy – the family. The next level: locality should include much fewer requirements and correspondingly decision-making because it is about periodic resource allocation and rules of cooperation, rather than the multitude of everyday activities. Likewise, the least number of requirements and decision-making should be at the state level because it covers more people and, therefore, more complexity, making it impossible to reconcile various **Desired Parameters of Existence.**

Another important reason is that the lower-level groups would be more effective in activities due to individuals' participation in decision-making, resulting in high levels of internal motivation and efforts. The individuals in control of higher-level groups' decisions make them without the involvement of the majority that is not in control. These decisions could be contradictory to an individual's wishes, therefore being resisted passively or actively. With the number of groups increasing with each lower level of the Hierarchy, somewhat polar approaches exist: treating all individuals as equal or treating individuals as primary members of groups with unequal rights and access to resources depending on a variety of privileges assigned to these groups from the top.

In an equal treatment option, one must accept the individual right of free association or disassociation, leading to flexible formation and dissolution of small groups with different sets of rules but a solid and resilient complex group with a few rules. Moreover, because individuals will direct their efforts to find or form a group, which would be most helpful for them in moving from **Perceived to Desired Parameters of Existence,** they would not care that much about other groups' decisions and actions as long as they generally have little impact on their activities and lives. And, since the decisions of individuals in control of the higher levels complex groups have limited scope, members of lower levels would not care about these decisions that much either.

In the group primacy option, one must deny the individual right of free association or disassociation. However, this denial would lead to the formation of rigid groups to which individual belongs under non-modifiable parameters, so the only way to move from **Perceived to Desired Parameters of Existence** is by extracting more privileges for one's group at the expense of others. The inevitable result would be continuing war, generally cold, but often on the brink of hot, for control of higher-level decision-making, consistently undermining cohesiveness or even the existence of the complex group.

INFERENCE: _The most important thing that one must remember is that any group of people, small or large, is not one entity but a network of thinking, feeling, and acting entities: human individuals. Humans could not survive outside of a group. Therefore the interactions of the individual with other members of the group are among the most important factors defining any individual's survival. Such interactions result in various resource allocations to individuals and their coordinated activity. Consequently, seemingly unified group action, in reality, is always just a combination of actions conducted by individuals with one and only one possible objective - to improve their future parameters of existence as they see fit. It does not change with the increase in complexity of the group; it just adds additional layers to interactions._

Part IV. Conceptual Understanding of Previous Development
Common Inheritance – Becoming Human

Once upon a time, some 3 to 5 million years ago, several various groups of hominins did something unusual that so far, no other animals did: they start calling each other names. In other words, they linked some vocalization to individuals. Then they proceeded to connect thousands of various specific combinations of sounds and gestures to all objects they could see around, characteristics of these objects, events, actions, and even things that existed only in imagination. This language creation allowed using the sequences of sounds to refer and describe non-present objects, previous experiences, and even plans for the future. Overall, it enhanced the complexity and value of interactions between individuals. The colossal consequence of this was human ability to transfer general information and technical knowledge and skills via a combination of language and demonstration, making such transfer a lot more effective and efficient than demonstration only, usual for non-linguistic animals. Moreover, it also allowed the transfer and accumulation of information in the form of stories and instructions, providing a continuing increase of the entire knowledge database, both general and technological, distributed in bits and pieces between the multitude of individuals. In short, these hominins created **Common Inheritance -** the powerful multiplier of their efforts to obtain necessary resources from the environment because it supports highly organized, planned, and coordinated actions directed at the goal defined by one or few individuals that agreed on this goal.

The important thing is that whatever this goal is, for example, it could be at the level of "let's hunt a big animal," the multitude of tasks necessary to achieve this goal had to be divided between individuals. These individuals would conduct their tasks under self-control, according to their knowledge, experience, and personal qualities. They also must reconcile individual objectives to improve the parameters of their existence with the shared goals of all group members. For example, a typical hunting technic is to use multiple individuals to create noises and images in such a way as to direct a big animal to a trap or ambush where some other individuals would kill the animal. The specific role of everyone would depend on the combination of individual characteristics: sex, age, previously demonstrated patterns of behavior, and such, with results unequally impacting personal standing in the group even if material results are divided equally.

The evolution resolved this need for reconciliation via developing the **Meaning of Existence Level**, which provides individuals with the definition of their proper role in coordinated activity based on indoctrination into cultural and ideological mores of this particular group. These mores leave an individual with some limitation of freedom, but it could not be consciously recognized because there are very few options to choose from anyway. Therefore, it is doubtful that individuals could deviate too much away from the group's very limited ideological and cultural mores. Furthermore, individuals could not possibly know any other set of rules, and it is not easy to invent new ones and convince others to accept them. However, individuals can and do introduce some small incremental changes guaranteeing cultural evolution, albeit relatively slow.

Overall, the prevailing attitude of people to each other had to be generally egalitarian, obviously adjusted for age and sex. The humans at the time lived in small groups, busy extracting resources from Environment, enjoying life when such resources were plentiful, and trying to survive periods when resources became scarce. There was little to exchange with or take away from others, even if understanding that something could belong to somebody was quite common. During this very long period, continuing cumulative development of Common Inheritance provided a powerful tool to adjust to changing environments that occurred either due to climate variations or movement to different environments. Eventually, humans populated the whole planet using different types of clothing, shelters, resource extraction technics, modes of behavior, and so on.

The Invention of Ownership and Hierarchy

Some ten thousand years ago, Humanity moved to the next step in its development. This next step was discovering that humans can somewhat control the environment by consistently selecting preferable specimens of plants and animals for human needs. This activity over multiple generations produced the modified species fit for survival only under human control, rather than in the natural environment. Correspondingly human survival got to be dependent on these species. This development created a foundation for agriculture when mutually domesticated plants, animals, and humans were dependent on each other to maintain specific environments that would not occur without human activities. Furthermore, the transfer to such a partially controlled environment, with its higher output of less-perishable goods, allowed humans to produce more than they would typically consume. As a result, they could save surplus, whether in the form of grain good enough to store for years or cattle that could be living under human control, or meat and fish that, if salted, dried, or smoked, also could be saved for a long time.

This surplus created a new layer of human interaction with Environment – identifiable assets. Such assets would include all conceivable resources usable for production or consumption that could have some formal title or informal recognition based on their quantitative evaluation and associated with an individual's name or identifier of a group. Something like "the land between lines linking these 20 stone marks belong to Paul" or "these two cows belong to Peter." This association also included cultural patterns added to **Common Inheritance** that expanded and somewhat formalized the direct control by some individuals over assets, so only Paul could decide what to plant on this land and, after harvest, use whatever he reaped. At the same time, only Peter could milk his two cows or butcher them for meat. Moreover, it allowed assigning value to services. In our example, if Paul, the plants' grower, would have some spare time between plant growing activities, he could use this time helping Peter with his cattle growing activities in exchange for milk or meat.

The invention of assets opened two new opportunities:

1.   Use **Ownership** Interaction & Cooperation method to exchange assets for some other assets: If Paul thinks that Peter's cows have more value than his land and Peter believes that Paul's land has more value than his cows, they could swap their assets. The most interesting in this transaction is that they both could be right. Because all human individuals are different, it is quite possible that Paul, who has land, hates plowing and harvesting but loves taking care of cows. In contrast, Peter, who is not that good with animals and hates to milk his cows every day, would be happy with the activities required to get most of the land. Therefore, the consequence of exchange would be more grain obtained from the same plot of the land by Peter, while Paul's loving care of cows would produce more milk. This exchange necessitates creating such rules of human interaction that would protect individual control over assets and freedom of action in their use, which means property rights. It also requires quantification of goods and services subject to exchange, eventually leading to the appearance of money as the unit of measure. Consequently, archeology finds plentiful evidence of trade as a voluntary exchange of goods and services going way back before any recorded history.

2.   Within the same timeframe, humans created another method of Exchange and Cooperation— **Hierarchy**, the organization of humans for taking something, either assets or services, without giving something in exchange. This invention happened when some individuals figured out that one could control agricultural production output from some territory, and even better, force some other people to work on this land. If successfully coerced, these other people would produce enough resources for their everyday survival and surplus that could be invested into military conquest, getting more land or cows. Depending on environmental conditions, Hierarchy could be as much or even more productive as Ownership, but differently. Instead of maximizing productivity via highly incentivized individual effort, it maximizes output by making massive improvements in land productivity via irrigation, terracing, and other enhancements, with slaves or workers being expandable during these efforts.

These developments logically led to intermixing of both methods. What is the point of growing grain or raising cows if somebody will come and take it from you? So, whatever you do, you must join others in some Hierarchy to protect your land and your cows, at least periodically, when a threat arises. But, on the other hand, if you are very good at fighting and robbing, have a decent Hierarchically organized gang, and can take everything from others and force them to do whatever you want, these activities would produce better returns than anything else. However, you still depend on the need for plants to grow and cows to be milked, even if you have no knowledge, skills, or intention to do any of this. Consequently, it would be best if you let people, who are growing and milking, not only stay alive but control the land and cattle, and do whatever they know how to do, so you can take your share of their product without interrupting production.

The intermixing of methods lasted for a long time, generally with an increase in complexity of tools and processes used in production and war, with either the Ownership or the Hierarchy becoming more dominant in various societies. In some cases, when the community can temporarily mobilize an effective military Hierarchy, the main functionality of society is maintained by using the Ownership method. For example, the ancient Greek democracies could mobilize from land-owning hoplite citizen-soldiers a military force good enough for protecting their city-states. Another example is the early American Republic, when the militia was good enough to fight Indian tribes, albeit not regular British troops. This militia came from the population that lived in main on farms or in small towns, was highly culturally diverse, armed, and, a crucial factor: the majority of active individuals were actual or inspiring Owners: either farmers or business people or apprentices. All these facts made the permanent Hierarchy impossible at the time. These societies combined limited but stable Hierarchy with individuals at the top selected via the somewhat democratic process.

However, a Hierarchy would often become dominant because it was more effective as a military power. It would also work better when environmental and technological conditions made massive use of simple labor, a relatively effective tool of top-down control over slaves or laborers. Thus, overall, throughout recorded human history Hierarchy method was generally dominant. However, it was not a simple process, and it lasted for a very long time.

The Hierarchy method also has a critical weakness: it becomes harmful to productive processes when it is too dominant. These processes inevitably use the formal or informal Ownership method. They suffer when individuals at the top of the Hierarchy override the decisions of Owners. The resulting deprivations from time to time caused people at the bottom to rebel. Consequently, the individuals at the top of the Hierarchy had to limit Hierarchy's dominance to stay alive and keep their group productive.

Many societies nicely demonstrated these dynamics when, even with extensive use of the ultimate Hierarchy of slavery, the slaves could buy their freedom from their masters. Of course, formally, it does not make any sense whatsoever because even if an individual's body belongs to somebody else, then all possessions of this individual also belong to this somebody else. However, informally, it makes sense because, while a slave formally does not own his body, he controls it. The consequence is that, even if the master could force the slave to do some simple tasks, it is pretty difficult to force people to do complex tasks if they do not want to. The catch is that the complex functions produce more and higher quality resources. So, if the master provides incentives for the slave to do complex tasks in exchange for freedom, the net result would be the paradox of the master making more out of the slave's labor by selling slaves to themselves and setting them free.

The Invention of Machines – Human Efforts Multiplier

After many thousand years of dynamic equilibrium between Hierarchy and Ownership, when the dominance of Hierarchy in its various forms continued unabated, it was slowly undermined by all kinds of technological developments, mainly in the military area. If individuals at the top of the Hierarchy ignored the latest and greatest military technology developments, they had an excellent chance to be taken over by their neighbors. Another driver for technology development was conspicuous consumption of top layers of society, which required luxurious goods and services. These conditions necessitated specialization of productive activities, development of complex processes with intermediate products, and expansion of trade in goods and services. In turn, it led to an increase in power of individuals who owned themselves and some set of resources that they could use enthusiastically and innovatively while being assured that they are at least somewhat protected from robbery. These people concentrated in cities where they established new forms of societies with their preferable rules of the game:

- The property rights assure an individual's ability to protect tangible property, including one's own body.
- Human rights assure the protection of intangible property, including the content of one's mind and the ability to express this content to others.
- Finally, the rule of law assures an individual's ability to use the Ownership method of Exchange & Cooperation and restricts the use of the Hierarchy.

These new arrangements first became dominant in Europe and North America in the XVI-XVII centuries. And then, by the end of the XIX century, all over the world, due to military superiority based on much more effective technology they produced compared to other countries where the Ownership method was more restricted. Over the following decades, individuals in countries where they were owners of fruits of their efforts invented chemical energy, mass-production tools, and much more effective tools designed to kill people. Nevertheless, hierarchy did remain dominant overall, running vast empires of the late XIX early XX century. However, this dominance was relatively light. Western societies in Europe and North America generally accepted the

Ownership's rules by supporting property rights, human rights, and the rule of law, even if these were quite limited.

During the same timeframe – the last 300 years, the significant change occurred in the human ability to generate new resources. The environment of intellectual and practical freedom brought in by temporary semi-dominance of Ownership method in some countries produced the industrial technology that started substituting human manual efforts with machines. Basically, it came down to this: individuals inventing technology that would allow making something that people need with a lot less human effort could implement this technology, produce this something much cheaper than it could be done before, sell it at a much lower price in much more quantities, and get lots of profit. Another critical ingredient was the limitation this environment imposed on the local lord or politician, denying them the ability to commit robbery against inventors or put them in prison for violating some artisan guild rule or hurt in any other way.

The new machines and production processes required more cooperation, implemented via business Hierarchy. Consequently, even if people benefited from better resource availability, they were damaged psychologically because industrial production methods deprived them of self-control derived from being productive Owners of resources such as land or shop. Instead of this, they had to forfeit their Ownership of newly non-competitive resources, join at the lower levels of some Hierarchy with somebody else at the top, and do routine, dull, and often unhealthy work under somebody else's control. This situation led to the new rearrangement of the population into various layers:

Sitting above everybody else were those who inherited or obtained a high position in the Hierarchy of government: various politicians, top-level government bureaucrats, and aristocrats in some countries. Next to them were the Owners of Human or Material Capital of such value that put them into upper layers of some corporate or political Hierarchy or, in rare cases, provided high returns on Individual Human Capital. These were individuals with big inheritance, top bureaucrats and politicians, the upper crust of the cultural establishment, and others in relatively unique positions.

The next layer represented most of the population - its middle class, which included Owners of Human and Material Capital of medium value that could provide returns sufficient for an acceptable lifestyle: small business owners, professionals, highly skilled workers, and individuals with competitive skills in various corporate Hierarchies.

Finally, at the bottom were the Owners of such a low level of Human and Material Capital that could not provide returns sufficient for supporting an acceptable lifestyle. Initially, it was a small share of the population. However, with the mass implementation of machines that substituted the Human Manual Capital, it began to grow at the expense of middle-class individuals with devalued Human Capital.

The population, except for the people at the bottom, generally accepted arrangement of society based on semi-dominance of Ownership method, even if they constantly haggled between themselves for resources:

1. The politicians and top-level government bureaucrats were always trying to snatch more resources under their control using taxes and regulations from the Owners of high-value Capital who controlled production and distribution. In turn, the Owners of high-value Capital were always trying to obtain support and protection from political Hierarchies, whether it is friendly legislation and executive action, suppression of competitors, or protection against law enforcement.

   The individuals in this upper layer of society are always corrupted and could not be otherwise, typically creating a symbiotic relationship when people move between business and political Hierarchies. However, the environment of unlimited freedom of speech and elections with secret voting protected from manipulation could keep the corruption of these individuals within reasonable bounds.

2. The Owners of mid-value Human Capital constantly play out on competition between the Owners of high-value Material Capital in the form of corporations and businesses, who always need practical help and therefore have to provide sufficient compensation to retain people who can supply it. But, quite often, such mid-level Owners also possess adequate levels of Material Capital so they can run a small business to provide competitive goods and services.

   As long as these individuals rely mainly on Human Cognitive Capital, the advance of technology that makes Human Manual Capital redundant does not bother them that much, except when increased productivity massively depreciates their Material Capital. Thus, for example, the independent tailor could not effectively compete with mass production factories on price, even if he provides better service and better products. So such tailor has to close the store and get a job at the factory, losing not only the Material Capital of the store but also seeing his Human Capital of tailoring skills depreciated to nothing and consequently finding himself at the bottom. However, an independent doctor or engineer would not care much about mass production because they control their complex activities, not somebody externally. As long as machines are just multiplier of human efforts, these people are always required and difficult to substitute with anything else.

3. Unlike all others, the Owners of low levels of Human and Material Capital found the advancement of productivity via machines implementation very harmful. Historically these were the people who used to work on the land as farmers or in small shops as

artisans. They were the foundation of production before, but now, human efforts multiplied by machines became so productive that the demand for these people went way down. To put it simply, if the same amount of goods and services that used to require 100 people to produce in the past now need only 20 people, then there are some 80 people that are redundant due to machines implementation.

American society found an imperfect solution during the early stages of the XX century. The answer was to decrease the Ownership method's application by expanding the use of Hierarchy and imposing limitations on production efficiency via unions, regulations, inspections, or whatnot. Another technique was confiscating produced resources from Owners by state Hierarchy and transferring these resources to individuals redundant for production. The members of the state Hierarchy used a variety of welfare programs and make-believe jobs created within the government to achieve this objective. Sometimes they even manage to shift the whole industries under government control, away from the Ownership method and consequently turning them into expensive producers of non-competitive low-quality goods and services.

Such accommodation worked relatively well, but it was far from enough. The redundancy impacted not only working people but also lots of individuals who obtained formal education that did not assure levels of Human Capital sufficient to support their preferred lifestyle. It was not even material returns that were lacking, but psychological need to be in control. It is not incidental that many late XIX and early XX century revolutionaries came from lower aristocratic or upper-middle-class backgrounds. These people could not wholeheartedly accept some middle-level supervisory position reporting to some uncouth business owner whom they consider way below themselves intellectually and morally.

These individuals developed pseudoscience of socialism – utopian organization of society as universal Hierarchy that includes the totality of people and eliminates Ownership method of exchange and cooperation. These people were expecting to obtain high-level positions within the Hierarchy because they were so intelligent and sophisticated that they knew all answers to all questions. They also believed that their decisions would be perfect or, at least, much better than could be done in a chaotic world of Owners' competition. Generally, history demonstrated that both suppositions were wrong. Low productivity of the public sector elsewhere in the world could attest that many answers were wrong and ideas unworkable. Likewise, the millions of skeletons of people with diplomas and degrees in deserted places of Soviet, Nazi, and Chinese concentration camps could attest to the low value of education as a survival tool in socialist Hierarchy. The extreme deviations from the Ownership method to the totalitarian Hierarchy method in various authentic implementations of socialism typical for the middle of the XXth century in many countries failed miserably. By the end of this century, they were mercifully behind.

Eventually, the equilibrium was established with the dominance of state Hierarchy controlled by public sector bureaucrats and politicians corruptly intertwined with multiple corporate Hierarchies controlled by "private" sector bureaucrats and politicians, and subordinate, but still productive massive use of Ownership method either in the form of small businesses or in the form of internal processes based on Human Capital inside big corporations. As a result, contemporary society generally satisfies the needs of individuals with uncompetitive Human Capital by providing positions at lower levels of Hierarchy and via welfare transfers.

This equilibrium is pretty shaky for two reasons:

- First, quite a few individuals with mid-level Human Capital find it hard to obtain resources and psychological satisfaction via the Ownership method. They could redirect their efforts from the struggle to find new and more effective ways to produce goods and services to the fight for better positions in some Hierarchy that would provide higher availability of resources and even better psychological satisfaction. However, such efforts redirection would decrease the amount and quality of resources produced. Moreover, if the speed of such transfer exceeds productivity growth, there would be fewer resources to redistribute.
- Second, in complex societies, such as the USA, which have high levels of genetic and cultural diversity, the competition for the places in Hierarchy that provide resources coercively taken from others is far from benign. It prompts people to form groups based on genetic and cultural commonality to be more effective in squabbling for privileges. These groups create additional tensions within society, eventually undermining its viability.

Despite this shakiness, this equilibrium continues so far, but it would not probably continue for much longer because of the constant increase in productivity. Moreover, this equilibrium likely will fail with the implementation of Artificial Intelligence (AI) capability that is getting ready to push humans out of producing generic goods and services.

The invention of Automation – Human Efforts Substitution

The new Artificial Intelligence (AI) technology is the latest addition to already existing technologies of automation that developed along with the implementation of a multitude of machines that had been making humans increasingly redundant for the production of goods and services. However, this addition is different from all other technologies because humans do not need to control AI directly or algorithmically to obtain the desired result of an action. Instead, AI acquires experience similarly to humans by going through many examples and linking inputs with desirable or undesirable outputs. Thus, the difference comes down to this:

- For humans, education, life, and professional experience create some specific configurations and conditions of biological neural networks in the human brain that allow them to produce some desired result, whether it is scratching one's nose or writing a new symphony.
- For Artificial Intelligence(AI), the massive data processing about inputs and outputs, desirable and non-desirable, creates specific sets of coefficients for multiple equations that imitate neural networks. These equations provide for AI's ability to achieve both types of desired results: either scratching a nose or writing a new symphony, which had already been demonstrated. The only key difference is that AI does not really have a nose or enjoy symphonies, so a human with a nose or love of music should initiate this action.

It now looks like humanity arrived at an inflection point where the development of **AI** makes most people redundant for producing goods and services. However, it does not entirely remove humans from the production process, leaving them with only one crucial role: to decide what kind of goods and services they want and preferences that would define tradeoff between different wants. There will also be a place for humans to invent new goods and services by generating unique, previously unknown needs and wants. These activities will always remain under human control because humans could never recede control without ceasing to be humans.

So, the question before humanity is which of two options is preferable:

1. Continue on the current path of development until the establishment of dominance of the **Hierarchy** method, with its protection of place in hierarchy and suppression of human and property rights, until decisions of individuals at the higher levels of Hierarchy define the lives of just about everybody.
2. Change the direction aiming to establish the dominance of the **Ownership** method, with its protection of tangible and intangible property, including human rights, until peoples' decisions control their lives within the scope of their resource availability. Obviously, they would have to reconcile their decisions with the others and optimize them with AI.

Part V. The Alternatives

World of Perfect Hierarchy Dominance

The humans tried to design and construct a society with complete dominance of Hierarchy many times, the latest and greatest being Soviet and Chinese forms of totalitarian socialism. These attempts always failed mainly because of the self-directing nature of human beings. It proved impossible to completely control an individual's actions, leave alone thoughts from outside. So, when put in a position of a small cog in the enormous hierarchical machine, humans still strive to achieve their desired parameters of existence, whether they are consistent with the desires of the superior cog in this machine or not. Consequently, the actual implementations of totalitarian socialism suffered from uncoordinated and often contradictory actions of individuals suffering from insufficient or even utterly absent ability to improve things by their efforts, rather than just complaining and waiting for that improvement will come from above. It also always featured massive corruption regardless of the severity of punishments and, overall, very low effectiveness combined with the mind-boggling level of inefficiency in all conceivable areas of human activities.

The arrival of Artificial Intelligence could change this and, for the first time in history, create the real material foundation for totalitarian socialism. Totalitarian socialism failed elsewhere before because it denied humans incentives to be productive. Thus totalitarian socialism is becoming viable in our time because AI can substitute humans in all production areas and even in trivial scientific research. Technically, it removes the need to apply Cognitive or Manual Human Capital for all practical purposes. Consequently, it means the real possibility of the unified Hierarchy managing all society's activities while producing effectively and efficiently sufficient amounts of goods and services for "bread and circuses."

This Hierarchy would combine a small human elite at the top with the enormous number of humanless productive cells controlled by AI and even a more significant number of non-productive cells populated by humans doing some make-believe jobs. The main objective of the human-populated cells would not be producing something, either goods or services. Instead, it would be allocating resources from the top down according to the wishes of elite individuals so it would satisfy their mainly psychological needs, such as exercising power over others. This future is neither utopia nor dystopia but rather a reality for a significant share of the population in the contemporary world. We already have huge, very busy, and well-compensated people who produce nothing of value, occupying cells in the big Hierarchies and entirely depending on the superior in the Hierarchy cog's good graces. These people are the "scientific" crowd that lives by the motto "publish or perish" and the bureaucratic crowd that lives by the slogan CYA (cover your ass). And the reality is that both groups are incapable of obtaining acceptable levels of resource allocation via voluntary exchange of goods and services.

With the advance of Hierarchy's dominance, it will become increasingly evident that it is unreconcilable with the individual freedom beyond the scope allowed for a specific cell in Hierarchy to which an individual belongs. Freedom requires the availability of resources in possession of the individual, something low-level cell occupants could not possibly have. The Material Capital will be unavailable because Hierarchy controls all material resources (socialism). Human Capital will be depreciated to the null because AI-controlled machines would be doing everything better than humans.

The big problem with such a society is at the top – the existence of power over others inevitably begets fights for this power, so elite at the top will fight each other, create coalitions, and do all the staff they had been traditionally doing since the invention of Hierarchy. It also means the indefinite continuation of switching between periods of stability and material prosperity when some strong individual(s) at the top control power and periods of misery and suffering when a few relatively equally matched conflicting coalitions fight for dominance. This fight at the top will always be supported from the bottom by individuals who are unhappy with the absence of freedom and seek to blow away the system and substitute it with something else, typically another Hierarchy, that they believe would provide a better deal for them. These individuals had always been wrong and will remain so.

World of Imperfect Ownership Dominance

Unlike Hierarchy, Ownership dominance could not possibly be perfect because all humans are different. Therefore their desired parameters of existence are always not the same for everybody, inevitably leading to situations when voluntary tradeoffs could not reconcile them. To resolve such cases, the use of at least some coercion would be necessary, requiring establishment and maintenance of law and order that only Hierarchy can do. However, since Ownership dominance means wide distribution of resources among the population as property, it would inevitably restrict the power of individuals at the top of Hierarchy via a variety of methods:

- Free flow of information supported by resources under the control of multiple owners who support different parties and ideas
- Formal division of power territorial: local / state / federal and functional: legislative / executive/judiciary
- Informal division of power derived from the massive distribution of resources between people that would guarantee impossibility to intimidate voters because they all have independent means.

- The absolute validity of elections because the individuals appointed by competing parties would control election process, rather than members of "non-partisan" Hierarchy

Another difference from Hierarchy dominance is that, while AI would also push people out of the production process, the remaining and critical function of decision-making will remain in the human hands, distributed among individuals. Thus, not top individuals in Hierarchy, but rather regular people will decide what goods and services produce and what tradeoffs to make based on their individual psychological and material needs.

The problem of inequality, if it is a problem, will never go away because individuals usually want to be something other than who they are and envy others who are closer to this. However, the opportunities presented by access to resources either directly or in coordination with others will significantly alleviate inequality. Everybody would always have at least minimally sufficient resource flow resulting from being a member of society qualified for a share of Common Inheritance. The individual ability to use this resource flow would support everybody's freedom to do something with one's life, whether to search for ways to amplify one's resources, enjoy arts or science, or even do nothing.

In short, the Ownership dominance, however imperfect, would support real individual freedom based on the extensive availability of resources created by the technological development of human society. At the same time, AI-controlled machines will substitute routine human labor, either manual or cognitive.

The Choice of The Dominant Method

So, the final word is simple: whether you are young enough and your life is ahead of you, or you are pretty old and care about what will be next for your children and grandchildren, or you just settled well in this life and do not care that much about the future, in either case, you have to choose one of three modes of behavior:

1. Do whatever you can to stop the advance of the Hierarchy method and make sure that the switch to the dominance of the Ownership method will occur. Then, you can hope that you and other people important for you will always have freedom and resources to act at will, rather than just complying with the choices of superiors in the Hierarchy. This lifestyle also includes the liberty of cooperating or not with others at will, rather than under duress.
2. Do whatever you can to support and advance the dominance of the Hierarchy method. You'll need to hope that you and other people who are essential for you will succeed in getting a good enough place in Hierarchy, so kissing up would not be too disgusting, and kicking down would be enjoyable.

3. Do nothing and enjoy your life as it is, hoping that whatever will happen will have no impact on your ability to do so.

I hope that enough people would clearly understand these options, choose option number one, and enjoy the future defined by this choice.

www.ingramcontent.com/pod-product-compliance
Lightning Source LLC
Chambersburg PA
CBHW061523250726
48657CB00005B/2033